Meath

≈ The Royal County ≈

Text by John Quinn

Paintings by Gerry Flaherty

Cottage

Publications

First published by Cottage Publications,
an imprint of Laurel Cottage Ltd.
Donaghadee, N. Ireland 2009.
Copyrights Reserved.
© Illustrations by Gerry Flaherty 2009.
© Text by John Quinn 2009.
Design & origination in Northern Ireland.
Printed & bound in China.
ISBN 978 1 900935 74 6

The Author

John Quinn was born in Ballivor Co. Meath in 1941 and spent the first fourteen years of his life in that village. He later lived in Navan for seven years. He taught at primary and secondary levels before becoming editor with an educational publisher.

In 1975 he joined RTE as an education officer before becoming a radio producer/presenter, which was his career for twenty-five years until he retired in 2002. In that capacity his radio programmes won many awards at home and abroad (Tokyo, New York).

He is also a successful writer. He has written six novels for children, one of which *The Summer of Lily and Esme,* won the Bisto Book of the Year Award in 1992. He has also written an adult novel, a personal memoir, *Letters to Olive,* and with Sean Boylan co-wrote the latter's autobiography *The Will to Win.* His childhood memoir *Goodnight Ballivor, I'll Sleep in Trim* was published in 2008.

He now lives in Clarinbridge, Co. Galway.

The Artist

Originally from Brandon on the Dingle Peninsula Gerry now resides in Navan, Co. Meath. He has had a lifelong interest in painting and drawing. Inspired initially by the spectacular and ever changing scenery in his native place, his work seeks to absorb the viewer in the mood and atmosphere of his chosen subject matter.

A self taught artist, his principal medium is oils and he paints in both representational and more abstract styles on a wide range of subjects incorporating landscape, seascape, wildlife and still life.

He has participated in numerous group shows and his work is included in corporate and private collections worldwide.

Gerry exhibits each Sunday at Merrion Square, Dublin and can be contacted at 087 2529295 or e-mail flahertyg2002@eircom.net.

Author Acknowledgements

I would like to acknowledge the assistance of Tom French of the Local Studies department, Meath County Library, and Tony Coogan for permission to use material from his book *Charlesfort – the story of a Meath estate and its People, 1668-1968*.

Contents

Welcome to Meath

What is Meath? Well, how long have you got? If you're in a hurry, here's the catechismal answer from the old geography textbook: *'Meath is the second largest county in the province of Leinster. Its chief towns are Trim, Navan and Kells ...'*. There is no point in listing the 'chief industries' of those towns as they are long defunct. That same textbook told us that Meath had *'no natural resources'* but it turned out that deep beneath its rich soil lay Europe's largest lead/zinc mine.

Such skeletal information tells us very little of the story of Meath. That story is a long one, dating back to the dawn of our civilisation, when our Stone Age ancestors cleared the forests of the Boyne Valley and settled into the farm-

ing way of life. They left behind them landmarks that enthral and puzzle us five thousand years later – the great passage tombs of the Boyne valley. We too easily equate Neanderthal man with savagery and ignorance, but these early Meathmen were builders, surveyors, astronomers and artists – and despite all our advances in learning and sophistication in enquiry we are still not sure what our ancestors were up to.

The geography books also told us that, being part of the Central Plain of Ireland, the landscape of Meath is flat. This is true, as the highest point in the county is less than a thousand feet above sea-level, but the few hills we have are among the most storied in the land. Tara, rising to a mere five hundred feet, is probably the most famous hill in Ireland. It became the great centre of power in ancient Ireland, becoming the seat of the High Kings. Once indeed, we were kings. Once indeed, we were a province – Midhe, the middle province, created by taking a slice of the existing Leinster, Munster, Connacht and Ulster. Later, in Norman times, we became a county. In deference to our regal past, we became known as the Royal County – a county with a proud tradition. Later still in medieval times, a part of the county was lopped off to form the new county of Westmeath, but we remained Meath, the Royal County.

The other little hills of Meath are equally storied. Loughcrew up in the north-west corner holds a cluster of Stone Age passage tombs within its womb. The Hill of Ward, near Athboy, is shrouded in magic and mystery. It was the site of a great pagan festival celebrating Samhain, the beginning of winter. Over on the hill of Slane, St. Patrick lit the Paschal fire in defiance of the High King and symbolically announced the coming of Christianity to Ireland. Four hills that in their own way tell much of the story of Ireland – from paganism to Christianity, from civil to church power.

'To Meath of the pastures
Go my cattle and me…'

So sang the drover in Padraic Colum's poem, confirming the image that most people would have of Meath. Lush grasslands divided into ranches of well-fattened 'beef to the heels' cattle. William Bulfin, travelling through the county in 1906, described it as *'a lovely wilderness of grass'*. For centuries Meath's grassland has been devoted to fattening cattle for the Dublin market. Young stock, bought at the great fairs of the west in Ballinasloe and Roscommon, were herded by train or driven by drovers to Meath's grassy plains. In my own native village of Ballivor there is a story of a legendary drover, who acquired the nickname 'Rooster' from his habit of sleeping in a tree while his charges grazed in a field below. The rich ranchlands of course connote a further image of wealthy Meath farmers, gruff and blunt in their dealings as they drive around in their four-wheel-drive jeeps. They do exist but they co-exist with many small-farm holders, labourers and part-time farmers.

Meath is not a county that would be readily associated with bogland but down in the south-west corner the Great Bog of Allen creeps over the borders of Offaly, Kildare and Westmeath into the Royal County. For over half a century, Bord na Móna has mined this natural source of energy in the Ballivor area. Even prior to their coming, a small army of soldiers descended on the bogs of Meath to cut turf during the 'Emergency' and supply it to essential services in Dublin. There is something haunting and lovely about a bog landscape. Ancient pine-trees bending to the constant onslaught of wind that sighs through their branches. Fragrant heather and bog-cotton dancing in the breeze. The exposed peatland scarred and streaked in black and brown, and pocked by dark and mysterious bogholes. The folk-memory of other days when turf was cut by hand and 'saved' with the help of neighbours. Memories of broiling hot sun, aching backs, ravenous hunger and glorious freedom. The bog represents only a small corner of Meath but for this writer it represents a place of unrivalled beauty and stillness, a sacred place.

And then there is the Boyne, the great regal river of Meath, practically bisecting the county and, together with its main tributary, the Blackwater, draining its fertile soil. An undistinguished river in its upper reaches, it is only when it reaches Trim that it attains the maturity and majesty it requires to mirror King John's Castle on its southern bank. Between Trim and Navan it acquires an elegance and grace that carry it through some of Meath's great estates. Swollen by the Blackwater it surges on Rhine-like through gorges and steep slopes to Slane. It is now a truly majestic river, broad in its sweep, sure in its flow, serenaded by poets and courted by anglers. Beyond Slane it courses in a dramatic loop – the Bend of the Boyne, which cradles the great passage-graves of Knowth, Newgrange and Dowth. Resuming its north-easterly course, it flows over the ford

on which two kings and their armies engaged in a momentous battle over three hundred years ago. It is the river of story. So many chapters of our history are etched in its meandering journey – Neolithic settlement, the coming of Christianity, Norse invasion, Norman conquest, dissolution of monasteries, Cromwellian destruction, Williamite war. It is the river of legend – its prize salmon was the source of all knowledge, accidentally conferred on a young boy. It is the river of great beauty, carrying itself with grace and serenity through a lush countryside.

The north-east corner of Meath boasts a wonderful natural amenity – twelve miles of coastline, much of it broad, expansive beaches at Bettystown and Laytown, where for centuries the people of Meath have sported and played in the summer months. In 1850 the beach at Bettystown gave up the magnificent Tara Brooch, an ornate and finely-worked treasure that dates back to probably the seventh century and which has become one of our national icons. History is never far away in the Royal County.

Some counties are noted for particular characteristics that are displayed by their denizens. Our next-door neighbours in Cavan are noted for their 'cuteness', for example. Is there such a thing as 'Meathness'? If there is, I suggest it lies in a droll humour uttered in laconic speech, with a drawling accent. Two examples, both football related, and no surprise in that.

• It is early summer 1992. The previous summer Meath and Dublin had enthralled the nation in a four-match saga. Meath eventually won and reached (and lost) the All-Ireland Final, playing ten matches in the process. So expectations were high in 1992. Unfortunately Meath were dumped out of the championship in the very first round by Laois. Two Meath farmers walk disconsolately from the scene. "Well Jimmy," one of them sighs, "there'll be no mastitis this year, anyway!" that is to say, last year we were so football-crazy, we forgot to milk the cows…

• About ten years later. Springtime. Meath are beaten by Kerry in a league match in Limerick. First appearance of the season for enigmatic Meath forward Ollie Murphy, who is not quite match-fit. Two Meath fans make their way out of the ground.

"What did you think of Ollie?"
"About two stone, I'd say."

That is to say he would need to shed a couple of stone in weight. In both cases, a sharp summation of the situation delivered with an economy of words. Meathness.

Football is a passion in Meath, particularly over the last few decades. Prior to that, Meath football had spent long spells in the doldrums, until in the early 1980s a little wizard from Dunboyne by the name of Sean Boylan took over management of the team, brewed up a mysterious herbal potion (or so the rest of the country believed) and for over two decades put the wind beneath the wings of his players. Success came often and it was good, but we wanted more. We were never satisfied. The greatest delight of all was in overcoming our arch-rivals from the capital, 'the Dubs'. The sight of their sky-blue jerseys released all our pent-up passions – not to mention those of the players – and a succession of notable jousts ensued, memorably the 1991 saga. Hard, uncompromising stuff. No love lost. No quarter given. It was 'manly' stuff and when victory came, it was so sweet. One problem for the supporters is the county's name. 'Meath' is too short to chant. It doesn't have the syllabic music of 'Galway' or 'Armagh'. 'Mee – eeth' sounds just awful, so we resort to reminding our opponents of our golden past. "Come on the Royal!" "You'll never beat the Royal!" Much better.

Place names are always a fascination, even if most of them are wayward anglicisations and corruptions. There is music in Moynalty (the plain of the flocks) and Crossakiel and Rathmolyon, but what is one to make of Girley, Trubly and Nobber? There is intrigue in Tierworker and

Seneschalstown and you will find Peru in the parish of Moynalty. And only in Ireland would the deserved winner of the Tidy Towns' Competition happen to be called Trim. Tidiness has nothing to do with the town's name of course. It is *Áth Troim,* the ford of the elder tree. Right next to that ford is the magnificent Trim Castle, the largest medieval castle in Ireland. It is the legacy of the Anglo-Norman baron Hugh de Lacy, who was given lordship of Meath by King Henry II. De Lacy's building programme in Meath would be the envy of many a modern developer and while most of his castles have crumbled over the centuries, Trim Castle remains a proud and majestic monument to Anglo-Norman construction.

Meath is of course about much more than battles and sieges – whether in Norman castles or in Croke Park. The Royal County can boast saints and scholars too. Nearly fifteen hundred years ago the scholars came 'from all arts and parts' (as Meath people would say) to Clonard to study under that university's founder, St. Finnian. It is not a mere flight of fancy to surmise that twelve hundred years ago a team of monks came together in Kells to produce a book that is one of the great artistic treasures of the world. In the seventeenth century that noble Loughcrew man, Oliver Plunkett, was martyred for his faith and raised to sainthood three centuries later. From the same Plunkett family came the prolific writer and patron of writers, Lord

Dunsany. He in turn took under his wing a young dreamer from Slane, Francis Ledwidge, who endured the horrors of the Great War and sang of the blackbird and the Boyne. Just down the road from Slane, the historic townland of Dowth gave us the poet and revolutionary, John Boyle O'Reilly. And over by Bective Bridge, Mary Lavin spun tales that still enthral us.

When the weatherman warns us of an approaching storm of "gale force-ten", we recall the Navan man who devised that scale of wind velocity, Francis Beaufort. This brilliant scientist also mapped many of the world's oceans as hydrographer to the British Navy.

Oh yes there is more to Meath than beef and football. Scholars abound – and, for some inexplicable reason, comedians too. Particularly in Navan, which has produced three contemporary ministers of fun – Dylan Moran, Tommy Tiernan and Hector O'Heochagáin. Is it the water? The air? The schooling? Who knows. And as for music, while,

the harp that once through Tara's halls
the soul of music shed

is now silent, the modern Boyne Valley still rocks to the music of minstrels such as Jagger and Springsteen, whenever Lord Henry Mountcharles opens up his back garden to the hordes at Slane.

Meath is a county of contrasts – rich pastures and lonely moors; a legendary river and lore-laden hills; antiquity and motorway; castles and ranches; abbeys and zinc-mines; scribes and no doubt a quota of Pharisees; saints and sinners too; scholars and farmers; footballers and High Kings. Welcome to the diversity that is the Royal County.

That diversity applies even more to the Meath population. Such is the mobility among people today that your neighbour in the sprawling estate of the commuter-belt is just as likely to come from Lagos as from Longwood, or from Killester as from Kilmessan. Meath is now totally within the commuter-belt. The fields and gardens that I played in as a child in Ballivor, thirty miles from Dublin, are now a jigsaw of housing estates, largely peopled by those who could not afford houses in the capital. This raises questions about identity. Counties remain administrative units, but in terms of population they have become a mixture of diverse cultures and origins. This can only be enriching for all concerned, but one wonders if decades from now there will be a 'Meath' at all. Will the Royal County have been subsumed into 'Greater Dublin'? And will that matter? Personally, I would miss the drawling accent, the laconic wit. Maybe I am wrong. Maybe a new sense of community will prevail and a new identity will be forged. Maybe sport will play a role in that. I have a dream. It is 2049. Meath have qualified for another All-Ireland Final, appropriately a century after their first victory. The hordes of fans assemble in Croke Park, waving their green and gold banners. Their forbears may have come from Vilnius or Cracow or Cabra, but as one they raise the proud old battle-cry – "You'll never beat the Royal!".

The hill of Tara, a few miles south-east of Navan, has been part of the weave of Irish history, myth and legend for thousands of years. While it only rises to a height of one hundred and fifty metres, it commands a panoramic view of the plain of Meath and its surrounding counties. One derivation of the name Teamhair is *'the place with a wide view'*. Another suggests that it was named after the Spanish goddess Tea.

Ancient texts list up to one hundred and fifty kings who reigned at Tara. They were never Kings of Ireland but Tara's sacred site (Stone Age people built a passage grave there four thousand years ago) and its lofty location gave them a sense of supreme authority. The legendary giant Fionn MacCumhaill and his band of mighty warriors, the Fianna, defended the High King against all invaders and performed amazing deeds of bravery and strength.

The modern visitor to Tara might think there is little to see at first. The best view is from the air. There is an audiovisual presentation in the former Church of Ireland, but even on foot it is possible to trace the great enclosure, the Fort of the Kings, and within it, Cormac's House and the Royal Seat. On Cormac's House stands the Lia Fáil, a magical Stone of Destiny which it was claimed roared out approval if the right choice of king was made. Nearby is the Mound of Hostages – the Stone Age passage grave. Outside the Fort of Kings are King Laoghaire's Fort and the Fort of the Synods, named after early Christian church assemblies. Further away is Gráinne's Fort. Gráinne was the daughter of Cormac MacAirt. She was betrothed to Fionn MacCumhaill but,

because he was ageing, she eloped with Diarmaid and the couple wandered Ireland for years before Diarmaid was killed by a boar. Near Gráinne's Fort are the Sloping Trenches, which look like two forts that have slid down the hill. The remaining monument consists of the two parallel trenches, thought to be the remains of the Great Banqueting Hall. Every three years a great gathering or 'Feis' was held at Tara. Laws were made, athletic contests were held and there was much music, storytelling and feasting – for which it was claimed it took *'thrice fifty steaming cooks'* to prepare the meals and three hundred men to serve them.

In more recent times Tara has flickered in and out of history. Realising its historical significance, local units of the United Irishmen staged a battle on the hill in 1798. Their ill-fated attempt led to the loss of four hundred rebels. In 1843 Daniel O'Connell also seized on the hill's significance when he organised one of his monster meetings there in his bid to repeal the Act of Union. In the twenty-first century Tara continues to court controversy. Despite much protest, a new motorway, the M3, is being built to run through the Tara-Skryne valley – too close to Tara's halls, the protesters say. Beneath the ancient hill, the heroes must be resting fitfully …

Tara

Clonard today is a quiet hamlet on the old Dublin-Galway road, now superseded by the M6. In the latter half of the first millennium, however, Clonard was a famed seat of monastic learning. The monastery was founded by St. Finnian around the year 520 AD. The annals tell us that Finnian had already been to Wales and France. Here close to the upper Boyne he set up his 'nursery of saints'. As Christianity rapidly expanded, other great men of learning – Ciaran of Seirkieran, Ciaran of Clonmacnoise, Brendan of Birr, Brendan of Clonfert and Colmcille of Derry – studied here before setting up their own monasteries. Finnian was a very pious man of great learning. He became known as 'Finnian the Wise' and attracted students not just from Ireland but from Britain and Germany. The annals tell of professors and contemplatives residing at Clonard and of a student body of some three thousand. While that figure may be an exaggeration, it does suggest that Clonard was a highly regarded and populous place of learning.

Unfortunately, Clonard was the repeated target of Danes, Irish chieftains and Normans. We are told that in 1045 *the town of Clonard, together with its churches, was wholly consumed, being thrice set on fire within one week*. Dermot McMurrough plundered Clonard in 1170. Little wonder then that there is not a trace of Finnian's monastic settlement today. Where once there were churches, cells and possibly a round tower there are now only the lush grasslands of Meath bordering the

Baptismal Font

Boyne. From a later medieval period there is a tree-topped motte (visible from the main road) and, in the local Catholic church, a beautiful carved baptismal font.

Given the lack of physical evidence, it is difficult to estimate the size and importance of the great monastic university that was Clonard, but maybe if we stand in one of the fertile meadows that gave it its name ('Cluain' is a meadow), close our eyes and listen – we might faintly hear on the breeze the monks chanting the praises of this great seat of learning.

Regressus in Clonardiam
Ad Cathedram Lecturae
Apponit diligentiam
Ad studium Scripturae

(Retreating to Clonard, to the church of instruction, he applied diligence to the study of scripture.)

St. Finnian's University, Clonard

Although it rises outside the county and enters the sea outside the county, the Boyne is Meath's river. Graceful, majestic, regal, its course bisects the county and, forming a Y with its main tributary, the Blackwater, it drains the entire county. It features in Ptolemy's 2nd century map of Ireland as Bovinda, named after the cow (bó) of a wise seer in Irish mythology.

Nobody has written better about the Boyne pursuing *the even tenor of its way*' than Sir William Wilde (father of Oscar) in *The Beauties of the Boyne and its tributary, the Blackwater* published in 1849. It is a rhapsody in prose, extolling the beauty and story of this great river.

'Beyond all doubt, the earliest kings of Erin reigned upon its banks, where also the earliest laws were framed, the earliest poems sung, and the most profound druidical mysteries celebrated. Soldiers and sages, bards and brehons have commemorated many of its localities; the romance of Irish history is laid amidst the scenery of this river, and much of the imagery of our earliest poets was drawn from this fertile source. The earliest abodes of learning and the most renowned schools of Christian philosophy had their seat by its margin; parliaments and councils were held in its castles; and

Wellington Monument, Trim

kingdoms – in battles fought by kings – were lost and won upon its banks...'

The Boyne rises near the Hill of Carbury in Co. Kildare and flows west in a great loop before heading off in its general northeast course through Meath. On its western bank are the ruin of Ballyboggan, once a great Augustinian abbey with five thousand acres and further north, the site of Tircroghan, once a mighty fortress until Cromwell's forces destroyed it in 1650. Near the village of Longwood the river passes under the Royal Canal which is carried high above the Boyne by a beautifully constructed aqueduct. A few miles on, Donore Castle stands sentinel over the Boyne. This is reputedly a 'ten-pound castle', built to specification to defend the Pale with a grant of ten pounds from King Henry VI.

In its upper reaches the Boyne is an unprepossessing river but, swollen by several tributaries, it reaches maturity as it approaches Trim. Just outside Trim it passes Newhaggard, a complex which includes a Georgian house, a six-storey mill and a guard-tower. The Boyne sweeps into the ancient town of Trim under a four-arched bridge which may stand over the original ford.

The Boyne

FROM SOURCE TO TRIM

Within a couple of years of the Anglo-Norman invasion of Ireland in 1170, King Henry II granted the Lordship of Meath to Baron Hugh de Lacy. De Lacy immediately built a fortification along the southern bank of the Boyne river at Trim. This was soon burned down by the invading King of Connacht, Rory O'Connor, but de Lacy replaced it with a more enduring fortress which would become the Trim Castle we know today. It is generally acknowledged as the finest specimen of Anglo-Norman military architecture in Ireland.

The site occupies over two acres and is contained within the Great Curtain Wall, which is nearly five hundred yards long and seventy feet high. The great keep or central tower within is rectangular with massive square towers abutting from each side. Some parts of the keep walls are twelve feet thick. The Curtain Wall featured ten protective towers and was further protected by a moat, filled with water diverted from the Boyne. The 'Dublin Gate' is in a barbican – a square protective tower – which would have featured a drawbridge, giving access to the circular tower within. If you were not a welcome visitor, access to Trim Castle would have been difficult indeed. No more than Rome, the castle was not built in a day, but over many years and in separate phases. During that time Hugh de Lacy was murdered (1186) and succeeded by his son, Walter.

When it was completed early in the 13th century, Trim Castle must have been an impressive sight. Surrounded by the moat it was in essence an island – and on that island it must have been the equivalent of a small town with living quarters for the lord and his retinue, visiting guests (who are reputed to have included Prince Hal – later Henry V – the Duke of Gloucester and Richard, Duke of York), soldiers, servants and workmen. There would be a great hall for feasting and entertainment. Parliaments and courts sat here. There would be a chapel and a prison and the underground vault housed the Royal Mint of Trim. A castle of this size and importance would be a busy and noisy place (especially when it was under siege!), but for de Lacy or subsequent occupants such as the Mortimers or Verdons, to climb the winding staircases to the topmost battlements must have given a commanding and exhilarating view of the plains of Meath and Kildare and beyond.

The castle is also known as King John's Castle. King John did visit in 1210 to deal with some of his troublesome barons, but the story goes that Walter de Lacy locked the place up and left town, leaving the king to camp outside the walls before returning to England! For all its might, Trim Castle had been largely abandoned by the end of the 15th century. Cromwell's troops damaged it further in 1649, but even in its ruined state we can only marvel at what an imposing place it must have been at the height of its power. Film-maker Mel Gibson helped us realise that image when he used Trim Castle as a location for battle-scenes in his 1995 film *Braveheart*.

Trim Castle

Regardless of the direction from which you approach Trim, a glance at its skyline will readily explain why it is a 'heritage town'. Mighty castles, ruined priories and abbeys, imposing monuments – Trim is truly steeped in history. It had been an important pre-Christian site before St. Loman sailed up the Boyne in 433 AD and built a church there. Both church and state centred a lot of power in Trim. South of the River Boyne stands the political centre, the magnificent Norman fortress, King John's Castle. North of the river is a line of monastic settlements stretching from the medieval St. Mary's Augustinian Abbey opposite the castle to the ruins of the Cathedral of St. Peter and Paul in Newtown to the east. History comes alive when, on leaving the castle, you cross the surging Boyne by the Millennium pedestrian bridge and walk the road that medieval pilgrims would have taken.

At the top of a ridge is the Yellow Steeple (so-called because of the colour of its stone in sunlight), the forty-metre ruin of the bell-tower of St. Mary's. Beside the steeple is Talbot's Castle, a 14th century manor house, still occupied. This was once a school whose students included the Duke of Wellington, MP for Meath and later conqueror of Napoleon (he is commemorated across the river by an imposing column) and the famed mathematician William Rowan Hamilton. Talbot's Castle was also once owned by Esther Johnson, known as 'Stella', the great friend of Jonathan Swift who had a parsonage at Laracor, a few miles south of Trim.

Back to the medieval road from St. Mary's to Newtown. You pass under the Sheepgate, the only remaining gate of five into the once-walled town of Trim. In the ruins of Newtown is the elaborate Elizabethan tombstone with its carved images of Sir Lucas Dillon and his wife, separated by the sword of purity! Just below the cathedral is another abbey ruin, beside the beautiful 15th century bridge. This is the remains of a hospital complex belonging to the Crutched Friars. What a busy place medieval Trim must have been! The Friars tending to the sick; the pilgrims making their way to St. Mary's to venerate the 'Idol of Trim' – a statue of the Virgin Mary. The modern pilgrim travelling from Dublin can stop at the Echo Gate (mind the traffic!), shout across the river and hear his voice rebounding from Newtown's wall.

Modern Trim is a fast-expanding business town within Dublin's commuter belt. For peace and solace, the pilgrim need only travel a little way out the Kildalkey Road to savour Butterstream, the enchanting garden created lovingly over twenty years by archaeologist Jim Reynolds. This series of gardens within a garden are in the words of Trim's motto *semper peregrino benigne* – ever welcoming to the traveller.

Trim

As it surges darkly and musically past King John's Castle, the Boyne acquires a majesty that befits its location. At Scurlogstown, site of a Norman settlement, it turns north and glides past the site of another Pale outpost, Trubly. William Wilde tells us that Cromwell slept in Trubly Castle the night after the siege of Drogheda. As it reaches Bective Abbey the river seems to burrow deeper, as wooded slopes flank its course. Just imagine drifting lazily on a punt under the arches of Bective Bridge and on past the Abbey's ruins. What stories might emerge!

Northwards towards Navan, the Boyne sweeps through the great demesnes of Balsoon, Bellinter, Dowdstown and Ardsallagh. Bellinter House, now a luxury hotel, was designed by the great architect Richard Castle for the Preston family. There is, as Wilde put it, *'antiquity as well as grandeur'* in these great Boyne parklands. In one of them, the modern Dalgan Park, the Columban Fathers built an imposing college in 1940 for the training of missionary priests for work in the Far East. As the river approaches Navan, two churches enhance its flanks. On the western side is the small medieval church at Cannistown which features several mysterious stone carvings. On the eastern side is the little church of Johnstown with its magnificent modern stained-glass windows and highly ornate baptismal font. Between the two churches the Boyne sweeps under the modern Kilcarn bridge, which replaced the beautiful eleven-arch 16th century bridge (hap-

The Robbing Bridge

pily still there for pedestrian traffic) and into Navan. The county town *'turned its back on the river'*, much to Wilde's disgust.

The Boyne passes under a mighty railway viaduct before joining its sister river from the north-west, the Blackwater. Just beyond the junction where the Boyne swings east is evidence of the river being harnessed for industrial purposes. A huge flaxmill was built on the riverside at Athlumney in 1806. As the Boyne heads for Slane the ruins of the 15th century Dunmoe Castle, said to be the home of the D'Arcy family, tower on its northern bank. Wilde compares the Boyne to the Rhine at this stage – *'high beetling crags, crowned by feudal halls and ruined chapels'* – but no sirens!. Certainly the view from Ardmulchan Church on the southside confirms this impression. Further upriver another lovely stone bridge, the Broadboyne, crosses the Boyne at Stackallen. Passing through *'the most delicious scenery'* (Wilde), the Palladian mansion at Beauparc is our next landmark followed by the Maiden's Rock or 'Lover's Leap' (maybe sirens at last). A little further on we meet Carrickdexter Castle, home of the Flemings, lords of Slane. We have reached Ledwidge Country.

The Boyne

FROM TRIM TO SLANE

Halfway between Trim and Navan, the Boyne glides majestically under a beautiful nine-arched ancient bridge and then past the ruins of a 12th century abbey and a medieval tower-house. This is Bective Abbey, a haunting silent witness to ecclesiastical history, civil power and, in the 20th century, literary prowess.

The original abbey was built in the middle of the 12th century by Murcha O'Maelseachlain, King of Meath, for monks of the Cistercian Order who had first come to Mellifont in Co. Louth. Murcha reputedly imported architects from Greece to oversee the project. Little remains of the original abbey but it would have followed the Cistercian plan of church, cloisters and outbuildings, surrounded by a demesne of several hundred acres. It was the scene of a bitter dispute over the remains of the great Norman baron of Meath, Hugh de Lacy, who was beheaded in 1186. His body was buried in Bective but the head was interred in St. Thomas's Abbey in Dublin. It was decreed that lands would be given to the abbey that held de Lacy's body, but which abbey would that be? A church court in 1205 decided in favour of St. Thomas's. A bizarre chapter in church history.

The present ruins date from the 15th century when the monks obviously felt under threat of attack. Lord Dunsany noted that,

'the holy men for whom it was built had fear of
grosser things than spiritual dangers, for though

they prayed in their chapels, they had battlements
on their towers, and wall of great thickness…'

When Henry VIII dissolved the monasteries, Bective came into the hands of one of his agents, Thomas Agard. He fortified it further, turning it into a manor-house and giving it the shape we see today.

Bective's literary association is with Mary Lavin, a prolific and polished short-story writer. Her first collection of short stories, published in 1942, was entitled *Tales from Bective Bridge*. Mary was born in the USA but her Galway-born mother pined for her homeland. When her father finally acceded to her wishes, by an extraordinary twist of fate he met the son of his American employer and the two went driving around Ireland. Mary told me the story in a radio interview in 1984.

"They happened to drive through a derelict estate of some three hundred acres in Bective, Co. Meath. 'Why don't you buy that estate and I will manage it for you?' my father suggested. It was done and that is how I came to live in Bective."

So over a period of eight hundred years Bective went from inspiring men of God to toil and pray to ultimately inspiring one of our most distinguished writers.

Bective

'Only an hour from Dublin' was the tagline of a 1970s radio commercial which hoped to entice city-dwellers to come shopping in Meath's capital. Twenty-first century commuters might beg to differ as they struggle to cope with increasingly heavier volumes of traffic. The county's capital has become part of the national capital's commuter belt.

The confluence of the Rivers Boyne and Blackwater was an inevitable site for an early settlement. A St. Fachtna is said to have founded a monastery here at Nuachongbhail (the new habitation). When the Norman lord de Lacy was given the kingdom of Meath, he had the town walled (hence modern Trimgate Street and Watergate Street). The de Angulo or Nangle family became Barons of Navan and had their residence to the south at Ardsallagh. Later through marriage the title passed to the Preston family (remembered in the former Protestant Preston School) and later still to the Ludlow family (as in Ludlow Street). To the west of the town is an ancient moat, traditionally the scene of many battles from prehistoric times to the era of the Norsemen. How the town derived its later name of An Uaimh (the cave) is still a matter of conjecture. In 1970 a plebiscite of ratepayers changed the official name to Navan.

Being surrounded by rich land and having access by road, water (the rivers and the Boyne Canal) and rail (links to Drogheda and Dublin) ensured Navan's growth as a market town in the 19th century. It boasted flour and flax mills and a distillery but in the twentieth century, it became more an industrial base. From its foundation in 1867, Clayton's Woollen Mills flourished for over a century. In 1938 Navan Carpets was established and became a market-leader for its high-quality product. The arrival of the Ailesbury family from Co. Offaly in 1880 was the foundation of a thriving furniture industry in Navan. When the Ailesbury factory burned down in 1927, several new factories were opened by former Ailesbury workers and Navan acquired a name for finely-crafted furniture. In 1970, a huge lead-zinc ore body was discovered on the fringe of the town and Tara Mines subsequently became the largest zinc mine in Europe. By the end of the century, Navan's industrial power had waned and today it is primarily an administrative centre and, increasingly, a dormitory town for Dublin as its boundaries extend and its population increases rapidly. Nowadays when Meath play Dublin, blue Dublin flags proliferate in the housing estates of Navan. Eight hundred years after de Lacy, another foreign invasion … Who would have thought?

A welcome recent addition to the arts life of the town is the Solstice Centre which features a theatre, art gallery, exhibition space and cafe. A busy business and shopping location, Navan is one of Ireland's fastest growing towns. The M3 motorway may bring it back to being 'only an hour from Dublin' – but that's another story.

Navan

Just beyond the confluence of the Boyne and the Blackwater at Navan stands the ruin of Athlumney Castle on the southern side of the Boyne. Originally built as a tower-house in the 15th century, it was expanded in later centuries by the Dowdall family. Nearby is the ruin of a 14th century church. The castle is an imposing pile of towers and gables, whose history is obscure and whose demise is poignantly recalled by William Wilde. It is said that Sir Launcelot Dowdall, on hearing the outcome of the Battle of the Boyne and the approach of the Williamite army, *'resolved that the Prince of Orange should never rest under his ancestral roof'*. He set fire to the castle and watched it burn from across the Boyne until *'with an aching and a despairing heart, he turned from the once happy scene of his youth and manhood and, flying to the continent, never returned to this country'*. To confuse us further, Wilde adds another tale to explain the burning of the castle at an earlier date. He tells of two jealous sisters who occupied the castles at Athlumney and Blackcastle (across the Boyne). Fearing the approach of Cromwell's troops, they entered a pact to burn both castles simultaneously. However, the scheming sister in Blackcastle only lit a brushwood fire in one tower and gleefully watched as Athlumney burned to the ground. It's a good story!

Donaghmore cemetery

A few miles east of Navan is the almost intact round tower of Donaghmore *(Domhnach Mór* – the great church). The ruin of a 13th century church is silhouetted beside it. The original monastic settlement is associated with St. Patrick who is said to have left his church in the care of his disciple Cassanus. The tower would have been built as a protection against the marauding Danes who came upriver from the Boyne estuary in 840 AD. The high doorway through which the monks retreated has a figure of the crucified Christ above it, with a human head on either side. We can only imagine the terror in the hearts of those holy men within the tower, as the dreaded longboats approached from the east.

South-east of Navan and across the valley from Tara is the hill of Skryne which derives its name from the Irish word *scrín,* a shrine. The relics of St. Colmcille were brought here from Iona in the year 875 AD. Prior to that, this hill was known as *Cnoc Ghuil* – the hill of weeping. In the third century, after the death of High King Cormac, there was a rebellion against his son Cairbre. He routed the rebels in a battle at the base of the hill, but was himself killed. His mother wept for so long over the loss of her son that the hill was named *Cnoc Ghuil.* At the top of the hill today stand the ruins of a medieval church from which there is a panoramic view of this storied countryside. In modern times Skryne's eminence as a football power has contributed such names as Trevor Giles, John McDermott and Colm O'Rourke to the pantheon of Royal County heroes.

A Castle, a Tower and a Shrine

Slane is said to have taken its name from King Slanius, one of five brothers who divided Ireland into five provinces. From the hill just outside the village there is great panoramic view of the storied landscape of Meath. Tradition tells us that St. Erc had a monastic settlement here and that in defiance of the High King, St. Patrick lit the Paschal fire on the hilltop to celebrate Easter in 433 AD. The present ruin is of a 16th century Franciscan friary built by the Fleming family, who were lords of Slane for five hundred years. There was also a college nearby which housed four priests, four lay-brothers and four choristers. Later the Capuchins came but were driven out by Cromwell.

The Flemings lost their estate during the Williamite War in the late 17th century. It came into the hands of the Conyngham family who originally came from Mount Charles in Co. Donegal – hence the family name of Mountcharles today. Their home, Slane Castle, dates from 1785. The architect James Gandon and the garden designer Capability Brown were among those consulted in its design. Famous for its round ballroom, the castle was host to many distinguished visitors over the centuries, among them King George IV of England, whose mistress was the Marchioness Conyngham. The present Earl, Henry Mountcharles, opened up the castle to the public for guided tours and special events – notably for the great summer rock concerts, when thousands of fans fill the natural amphitheatre of the grounds to enjoy the music of topline acts including U2, the Rolling Stones, Springsteen, Bowie and many more. A disastrous fire in 1991 closed the castle to the public but it was open for business again a decade later.

The village grew up around the estate and is dominated by four magnificent Georgian houses facing each other across 'the square', which today is the very busy intersection of the Dublin-Derry and Drogheda-Navan roads. You can take your pick of the stories of the origin of the houses. Were they built for four Conyngham sisters who didn't talk to each other or for the pillars of local society – priest, doctor, magistrate and constable? At the top of the village is a monument to local participation in the 1798 rebellion. Both churches in Slane – Church of Ireland and Catholic – feature stone fragments rescued from medieval churches in the area. The outstanding feature of the Church of Ireland church is the intricately-carved coat-of-arms of the Barnewall family above the west doorway.

For a small village, Slane has a high quota of artistic sons – poets Francis Ledwidge and John Boyle O'Reilly, and the Victorian artist John Cassidy. For William Wilde, the hill of Slane resonated with history, *'here, pilgrim, stop, rest on yonder monumental slab… The ground whereon we stand is sacred… Look abroad over the wide, undulating plains of Meath… where in the broad landscapes of Britain find we a scene more fruitful and varied, or one more full of interesting, heart-stirring association?…'*

Slane

Francis Ledwidge (1887 – 1917), the 'poet of the blackbird', is one of Meath's best-loved sons. He grew up in extreme poverty in Janeville, just outside Slane. One of a family of nine, his labourer father died when Ledwidge was only five and his eldest brother died when the poet was seven. He had only a basic education but read a lot of books acquired with the halfpennies he earned for running messages. Those books and *the songs and stories told at my mother's doorstep in the owl's light*' were his early inspirations. He left school before he was fourteen and worked at a variety of jobs – farmer's boy, grocer's assistant, road worker, clerk – to help his impoverished mother. He was an ordinary young lad – a passionate follower of the Slane Blues football team and a member of the local dramatic group – but also a dreamer.

Ledwidge had some early verses published in the *Drogheda Independent,* but, seeking a wider audience, he wrote in 1912 to another Meath writer, Lord Dunsany, for encouragement. Dunsany responded positively and became the young poet's patron, finding new outlets for his work and introducing him to other writers like McDonagh, Gogarty and Katherine Tynan. He got caught up in the political fervour of the time, being secretary of the local branch of the Irish Volunteers in the pursuit of Home Rule. Around this time the poet fell in love with Ellie Vaughey who would ultimately reject him, a rejection that hurt him deeply. To the surprise of many, Ledwidge joined the Royal Inniskilling Fusiliers on the outbreak of the Great War in 1914.

His first action was in the disastrous Gallipoli campaign. *'It was Hell! Hell! No man thought he would ever return.'* Here, improbably, he received a copy of his first book *Songs of the Fields*. *'It is a lovely book, but my best is not yet in it'.* Unlike the war-poets, Ledwidge was writing about nature, love and his beloved home county. *'Remember me to every hill, wood and ruin in Meath.'* His return home to recuperate from illness coincided with the Easter Rising of 1916 which resulted in the execution of his friend Thomas McDonagh:

> *'He shall not hear the bittern cry*
> *In the wild sky where he is lain'*

Poetry was always *'the thing that matters'* and on his return to action in France in December 1916 he wrote whenever he was away from the front line. The campaign in France was equally horrific. 135,000 Allied troops died in one day for a gain of one hundred yards. On July 31st, 1917 Ledwidge was killed by a shell while building a road to the front. Three months later, his second collection, *Songs of Peace* was published. A plaque in his memory was installed on the Boyne Bridge in 1962 and his cottage in Janeville is now a Ledwidge Museum.

Francis Ledwidge

The Boyne sweeps gracefully into Slane past the great castle of the Conynghams. It is now a majestic river, beloved by fishermen and poets;

Little waves put out their white tongues
Just beyond the mossy weir,
Where the jewelled trout are leaping
And the heron flings his spear.

(Francis Ledwidge)

The 'mossy weir' diverts water under the many-arched bridge to serve the great mill, built by David Jebb. When it opened in 1776, Jebb's Mill was the largest flour-mill in the country and after over two centuries in existence – later serving spinning, weaving and manufacturing industries – it is still relatively intact. Jebb's Georgian millhouse later became the Boyneville Hotel, serving passengers on the pleasure-boats that came from Drogheda in the 19th century. Across from the mill are the ruins of Fennor Castle, a 17th century house which was earlier the site of a medieval castle.

Near Rosnaree, said to be the site of King Cormac MacAirt's palace and his burial place, the river flows in a great curve, known as the Bend of Boyne. Here is the cradle of our civilisation, where Stone Age farmers cleared the forests and settled before building what Wilde called *'the great pyramids of Western Europe – Knowth, Newgrange and Dowth'.* The sacred landscape of Brú na Bóinne (Boyne Hall) is now designated a World Heritage Site and is a lasting tribute to the skill and art of our earliest ancestors. Across the river from Dowth is the Brú na Bóinne Visitor Centre at Donore.

As the Boyne comes out of its Bend and heads east for its final course to the sea, we come to another historic scene of more recent times, at Oldbridge. There was no bridge here in 1690, but a ford where two English kings and their armies faced each other. James II, a Catholic who had been ousted from the throne of England, was encamped with some 25,000 troops on the southern bank of the Boyne near Donore. On the northern bank, James' Protestant son-in-law, William of Orange, massed his 36,000 troops. William outwitted James by sending a pincer movement down from Rosnaree while crossing at Oldbridge himself. The Jacobites were beaten and James fled to France. It was July 1st, 1690 – later adjusted in the calendar to July 12th – the 'Glorious Twelfth' still celebrated by the Orange Order today.

The Boyne waters flow on out of history, out of the Royal County, through the ancient town of Drogheda under the magnificent new bridge and equally imposing railway viaduct and into the sea at Mornington.

The Boyne

FROM SLANE TO THE SEA

It is a warm June day in 1995. I am at the prehistoric site of Knowth on the bend of the Boyne. I am here with historian George Cunningham to record a radio programme for the series *The Mark of Man*. We are joined by the great archaeologist Frank Mitchell, who lives just across the Boyne in Townley Hall. Come with us on our exploration of Knowth.

George reminds us that we have not one but four stories here in Knowth – the first Stone Age settlers, Iron Age people from around 400 AD, then an early Christian settlement and finally the coming of the Normans. We stand beside the huge central mound – ninety metres by eighty metres, reaching to a height of ten metres. It is surrounded by a ring of tall stones which feature carved spiral and crescent designs. "Remember," says Frank, "these fellows had no metal, so they would have chiselled these designs with quartz. And as for the passage-tomb, we're not talking about a heap of stones thrown roughly together. The Stone Age settlers would have had the equivalent of modern quantity surveyors and architects. For the stone they needed prospectors and collecting parties. The quartz stones would have come from Wicklow and the granite from the Mournes…"

Frank Mitchell worked on the original excavation with Professor George Eogan. It began in 1962 but it was not until five years later that Eogan discovered a cavity which led him down a twenty-metre passage and into a central chamber, where stood a lavishly carved stone basin, a metre in diameter. I ask Frank if he can remember the first time he entered the tomb. "It was difficult to get in there because the passage walls were collapsing. The Stone Age people had lit a lot of fires in there. The walls were covered in soot, but what astounded me was the discovery that later Christian settlers had drawn figures in the soot with their fingers. We could still make out their doodles."

There are seventeen smaller satellite mounds surrounding the Central Mound in higgledy-piggledy fashion. To my delight we are allowed enter one of them. We squirm and worm our way down the passage. There is no central or side chamber at the end but it is an extraordinary privilege to stand at the end of the passage in a Stone Age tomb.

Outside, George reminds us that, mysteriously, there was no activity here for a couple of thousand years until the Iron Age people came, dug defensive ditches and lived on top of the mounds. "Later, the Normans came and found they had ready-built mottes to occupy. There's great continuity of history here".

"Indeed," adds Frank. "Look over there. That's the corner-wall of a 17th century farmhouse. They pinched some of the big stones from the tomb to build it!"

Knowth

This great Stone-Age burial-tomb dominates the Bend of the Boyne in the Valley of the Kings. We can only marvel at its construction and the amazing artwork on its stones. Who were its builders? Who was buried here? Why this location? So much is shrouded in mystery but it is clear that its location, design and orientation are directed towards the sun, marking in particular the winter solstice sunrise on December 21st. This huge mound, measuring approximately 12 metres in height by 100 metres in width, pre-dates both Stonehenge in England and the Egyptian Pyramids. It is partially ringed with kerbstones, some of which are decorated. The entrance to the tomb is marked by a huge intricately-carved stone.

The nineteen-metre long passage slopes upwards into a central chamber which has three recesses opening from it. The archaeologist M.J. O'Kelly began excavating Newgrange in 1962 but it was not until 1967 that he made the major discovery regarding the roof-box above the entrance. For a few days either side of the solstice, the rising sun's rays creep through the roof-box until they reach the centre of the chamber. This process takes nineteen minutes. Every year a privileged group gathers in the chamber at the winter solstice to witness this amazing spectacle. Spectacular photographs bear witness to the extraordinary skill of the builders of this mound five thousand years ago. They were skilful builders, manoeuvring huge wall-and roof-stones into position. They were marvellous engineers – the interior is still bone-dry today. And they were gifted astronomers, finding the perfect alignment of the solstice sun with their edifice. But the great mystery remains.

Why? What was their purpose? This was almost certainly a tomb but for whom? Was it a temple of some kind? Was the solstice light meant to be a comfort for those buried within, a reassurance in the dark of winter that there was an afterlife? Did the Stone Age people worship a sun-god? The mystery remains.

Inside the tomb as well as outside, the beautiful artwork enthrals us, notably the triple-spiral which has become the 'logo' of Newgrange. Again we must remember how primitive these artists' tools were. Was this art their language for expressing their belief in a sun-god? The arguments continue, as indeed they do over the re-construction that visitors see today. Whatever side they take, the visitors come in their thousands all year round to absorb the wonders of this World Heritage site. This is truly a sacred place.

Newgrange

Dowth is the most easterly of the three great Stone Age burial tombs in the Bend of the Boyne and while it was excavated as far back as the mid-nineteenth century, it is regarded as the Cinderella of the three tombs in terms of exploration. It comprises two passage graves – known as Dowth North and Dowth South – about twenty metres apart. Dowth North is a typical passage grave – a passage about twelve metres long leading to a central chamber with two side-chambers – and in this case two more small chambers off the right-hand side chamber. In Dowth South are many examples of passage grave art – various geometric designs pecked out with stone chisels by artists some five thousand years ago. What they signify is still a mystery, no more than the spiral designs (sunbursts?) on some of the huge kerbstones surrounding the mound outside. The plunder of the Danes in the ninth century would not have helped in solving the mystery

Thanks to the great water-colourist Gabriel Beranger we know that in the 18th century the eccentric lord of these parts, John Netterville, built a sort of temple on top of the mound at Dowth. This glorified tea-room had *a gallery which is to serve as orchestra*, according to Beranger. The 19th century excavations put an end to the tea-room, however. Sir William Wilde records that a few hundred metres to the south-east of Dowth *we have St. Bernard's Well; some remains of one of those structures denominated Giants' Graves; the old castle of Dowth; and the little church adjoining.*

There is a further historic connection with the Nettervilles. In the early 19th century there existed a Netterville Institute for orphaned children. A teacher on the staff here was the father of John Boyle O'Reilly, poet, patriot and journalist. A member of the Fenian Brotherhood, he actually joined the British Army to recruit soldiers to Fenianism. He was arrested in 1866 and imprisoned in Dartmoor. He escaped from prison, was rearrested and sentenced to penal servitude in Australia. Again he escaped by whaling ship and made his way to Boston where he became a very public figure and editor of the newspaper *The Boston Pilot*. Through the *Pilot* he campaigned against racism and anti-Semitism. He longed to return to the Boyne Valley and asked that he be buried under the spot where he had carved his initials on the wall of the old church at Dowth. He died and was buried in Boston in 1890, however, but the Dowth stone he had initialled was later brought to his tomb in Boston. His wish was granted and some fifty years later a monument was erected to his memory in the ruin of the old church in Dowth. It was said of John Boyle O'Reilly that *'Ireland gave him birth, England exile and America fame'.*

Dowth

The Irish name for Duleek, *Damhliag Chianáin,* tells much of the story of this settlement along the winding River Nanny, about four miles from Drogheda. Damhliag is a stone church and Cianán was an Irish monk, educated in France and reputedly a stonemason. Here on the banks of the Nanny Cianán built what is claimed to have been the first stone church in Ireland and attracted a large community of monks. The church is long gone but evidence of the monastic importance of Duleek can be seen in the existence of two 9th century high crosses (one incomplete) in the ruins of a later medieval church. These finely-carved crosses depict Biblical scenes and fabulous animals. There is also evidence that a round tower once stood here. The settlement was regularly plundered by the Norsemen. In Norman times an Augustinian abbey was established.

After the Anglo-Norman invasion the Bellew family acquired large estates in the area and are commemorated in the name Bellewstown, upon whose famous hill horse-racing has taken place for almost three hundred years. In the 19th century Bellewstown Races were considered an event of high fashion. One of the many interesting grave monuments in the medieval church commemorates John Bellew who *'was shot in the belly in Aughrim fight, the first of July 1691…'* A year earlier the ancient bridge over the Nanny had played a central role in the Battle of the Boyne. King James II mounted his cannons on the bridge to protect his retreating troops and ultimately to effect his own escape to France. A later royal visitor to Duleek was King George IV, who came in 1821 to Annsbrook, an eighteenth century rector's mansion. The King disappointed his host, who had gone to great lengths to embellish his house for the occasion. Being claustrophobic, the King insisted on dining al fresco – or so the story goes.

William Bathe and his wife Jennet Dowdall lived in Athcarne Castle and were obviously a very devoted couple. We know this because when William Bathe died in 1599, Jennet had a number of wayside crosses erected to his memory. These stone crosses of which there are numerous examples in Co. Meath, are inscribed with details of the couple's lives and a request to pray for their souls. Figures of saints and biblical scenes are carved on the crosses. These seventeenth century 'memoriam cards' have endured for centuries by the side of Duleek's ever-busier roads.

A colourful character menaced these same roads in the 19th century. This was Collier the Highwayman, who stalked travellers in these parts for years until he was caught and transported to Australia. He subsequently joined the British Army, made his way to the USA and from there returned to Ireland to end his days. Ironically, Collier collapsed and died at Bellewstown Races in 1849. Saints and sinners – Duleek has seen them all!

Duleek

The Royal County is blessed with twelve miles of coastline from the mouth of the Boyne at Mornington (where two ancient beacons – the Maiden Tower and the Lady's Finger – warn seafarers of dangerous sands) to Gormanstown near the Dublin border. For centuries the people of Meath have flocked to the expansive two-mile stretch of beach at Bettystown and Laytown to sport themselves in summertime. Laytown boasts a unique race-meeting on the strand, a moveable feast depending on the tides. Further south is Mosney which flourished as a holiday-camp in the 1950s. Later it became the venue for the national Community Games and later still an immigration centre. Bettystown and Laytown are now part of the ever-expanding Dublin commuter belt. An interesting development on the banks of the River Nanny is Sonairte, the National Ecology Centre. Set up by local people and committed environmentalists, it is run by volunteers and features an organic farm, a shop, information centre and nature trails.

Travelling inland along the Dublin border we come to Fourknocks, an elaborate passage-tomb which was excavated in the 1950s. A second mound nearby also disclosed a complicated burial monument dating back some four thousand years. Travelling on towards Dunshaughlin we come to Lagore, the site of a crannóg or lake-dwelling associated with the kings of Meath of over a thousand years ago. The town of Dunshaughlin *(Domhnach Seachnaill*, the church of Seachnaill) has the ruin of a 10th century church which features a crucifixion scene on a door-lintel. On the Dublin side of Dunshaughlin, Rathbeggan Lakes are a popular attraction for anglers. The city of Dublin or at least its workers have in recent years encroached greatly into this part of Meath. The once-quiet and almost remote village of Ratoath is now a rapidly-expanding satellite town. Ashbourne, likewise was, in living memory, a one-street village but is now a 'new town' or as it was described at the planning stage – a 'garden city!'

On the fringe of the town at a road junction stands an impressive monument on a crucifixion theme. It commemorates two republican rebels who died in an encounter with British troops and police in 1916. It was a pretty fierce encounter. Seven policemen and three passers-by died. The rebels were led by the local schoolmaster Thomas Ashe. A line from a poem of his is inscribed on the monument – *'Let me carry your cross for Ireland, Lord'.*

Crossing over to Dunboyne we pay tribute to the Connelly farmhouse at Flathouse. For fifteen years it was the best-known farmhouse in Ireland, being the location for the filming of RTE's ground breaking rural 'soap', *The Riordans.* As we cross the railway bridges and negotiate the sharp bends, we are reminded that these roads were a mecca for motorsport enthusiasts in the 1960s when the Leinster Motor Club staged its annual race-meeting over a four-mile circuit. Today, negotiating your way through Dunboyne's relentless city-bound traffic is a sport in itself.

East Meath

There are many Meath people who would argue that this attractive town on the Dublin-Meath border should be re-named Dunboylan in memory of its famous son Sean Boylan. Sean was manager of the Meath gaelic football team for an amazing twenty-three years (1982-2005) during which he brought extraordinary success to the county. Although Dunboyne is on the fringe of Dublin city it is equally in the heart of ranch country – witness the stud-farms and large cattlefarms that cry halt to the encroaching city. One of those farms belongs to the Bruton family, from which is descended other famous Dunboyne sons – John and Richard Bruton, Fine Gael TDs. John is former leader of Fine Gael and was Taoiseach of a coalition government from 1994 to 1997.

Sean Boylan's family is steeped in national history. His ancestors' home in Tara was burned to the ground by British yeomen following a skirmish which was part of the 1798 rebellion. Dunboyne suffered even worse in 1798. It was practically razed by the yeomen but it was to Dunboyne that Sean's ancestors moved. They built up a farming business there, but the family also carried with them a deep knowledge of the healing properties of herbs. This knowledge has been passed down through the generations and today herbalism is Sean's business. He farms herbs on his land and runs a very successful clinic and laboratory in the treatment of various ailments. Clients come from all over the country seeking treatment for a wide variety of ailments. Sean can point to a field now planted with parsley-piert and recall that it was originally Dunboyne's hurling field (Dunboyne won a string of county titles in the early 20th century) – but it was also the scene of a great Irish Volunteers' rally in 1917 when vast crowds assembled to be addressed by Michael Collins and Arthur Griffith. History and herbs surely rhyme in the Boylan story.

Although he came from a hurling background, Sean was asked in 1982 – to the surprise of many – to manage the Meath football team. It wasn't an exciting prospect. Meath had won only three All-Ireland titles in a century (the last one in 1967) and their fortunes were at a low ebb. But the Dunboyne healer built a team, managed and moulded them and devised seemingly eccentric training methods which were based on his astute knowledge of the human body. For the next twenty-three years he took Meath football on an amazing roller-coaster journey, achieving remarkable results – four All-Ireland titles, runners-up on three occasions, eight provincial titles, three National League titles, a Centenary Cup, a host of All-Star awards for his players and the undying gratitude of Meath football fans. He subsequently managed the Irish International Rules football team in their jousts with Australia.

Dunboyne

The Plunketts were a pre-Norman Irish family who acquired vast tracts of land in medieval Meath from Loughcrew in the north-west across to Dunsany and Killeen in the east. Dunsany Castle was built in 1180 by Hugh de Lacy to guard the Dublin-Trim road against *the savage Irish*. It was first held by the de Cusack family but passed to the Plunketts through marriage. Christopher Plunkett was appointed the first Baron Dunsany in the 15th century. Dunsany is one of the oldest continuously inhabited houses in Ireland and has a colourful history. In 1609 the wife of the 8th Baron was murdered. The murderer later confessed but only after the unfortunate Honora Caffrey had been burned at the stake for the crime.

Edward John Moreton Drax Plunkett (1878-1957) is the best-known Baron for his literary achievements – as a prolific writer of plays and novels himself and as the patron of Francis Ledwidge. The castle holds an extensive collection of family memorabilia; art, porcelain and weaponry collections and a vast library. In the grounds stands the ruin of the 15th century church of St. Nicholas.

To the east of Dunsany stood the other great Plunkett ancestral home – Killeen Castle, another Pale fortress built by Hugh de Lacy. Again, through marriage, Killeen passed through the de Granville and Cusack families to the Plunketts. In medieval times the Plunketts were noted for their religious fervour, many of them becoming abbots and bishops. Their tombs can be seen in the ruin of the 15th century church at Killeen. Sir Christopher Plunkett and his wife Joan Cusack founded a confraternity of brothers and sisters called 'The Guild of the Blessed Virgin' here and established a 'college' for the diffusion of religion and charity among the Catholic population. The great historian Dean Anthony Cogan tells of the privations suffered by the Plunketts in Cromwellian times. Dr Patrick Plunkett, Bishop of Meath, was living on the hills, in the woods and the cabins of the poor.

Killeen and the Plunketts survived the Cromwellians but would eventually succumb to their own countrymen in the 20th century. In her memoir *Seventy Years Young*, Elizabeth, Countess of Fingall, poignantly recalls waiting for the burners to come to Killeen during the Civil War in 1923,

'The cold dawn broke on Fingall and myself sitting shivering in the study ... 'I in my fur coat with my jewel-case on my knees ...' They won't come now, we thought. And we climbed stiffly and wearily up the great staircase to bed ...'

However, nearly six decades later the burners did come. In 1981 at the height of the H-Block hunger strikes, arsonists set fire to Killeen Castle and the ancient home of the Plunketts was reduced to a shell. The castle was restored and is today a hotel and golf resort.

The Plunkett Castles

The village of Summerhill owes its origin to Summerhill House, the stately home of Sir Hercules Langford. This was built on a hill-top which was originally the site of a castle owned by the Lynch family. (Hence the Irish name *Cnoc an Loinsigh* – Lynch's Hill). The modern village green was once part of the approach to Langford's mansion, which was designed in the 1750s by Richard Castle (or Cassells), a distinguished architect of German origin. He also designed Bellinter House, near Navan. Through marriage, Summerhill House came into the Rowley family. Hercules Langford Rowley, known as *'the incorruptible representative of Co. Meath',* sat in the Irish Parliament for fifty-one years. Ambrosio O'Higgins, Viceroy of Peru and father of Bernardo O'Higgins, liberator of Chile, is said to have grown up on the Summerhill Estate. Rowley planned the attractive village of Summerhill as it stands today. The mansion was badly damaged by fire in 1800. In the late 19th century Empress Elizabeth of Austria visited Summerhill House to participate in the hunting season. She was brought by special train to Kilcock and from thence to Summerhill by carriage.

Rowley's mansion was burned to the ground during 'the Troubles' in the 1920s. Today the avenue leads to a modern bungalow. Nearby are the ruins of Lynch's Castle.

In modern times Summerhill's most distinguished son is Mick Lyons, a great full-back for Meath gaelic footballers in the 1980s and 90s. Such was his strength and durability as a full-back, he was equally entitled to the name Hercules! Another Herculean Summerhill man, Gerry Smyth, won an athletics gold medal at the World Senior Games in Utah at the mature age of 97.

Over the past twenty years Summerhill has blazed a pioneering trail in its concern for older people and in the promotion of active ageing. What began as an Active Retirement Group is now the Third Age Foundation whose many initiatives have been developed nationally and internationally. The dynamic Mary Nally and her team keep coming up with innovative projects. Summerhill leads, the world follows!

An early settlement near Summerhill village was Dangan Castle, built by Sir Simon Cusack in the 13th century. It became the home of the de Wellesley family, whose most famous son, the Duke of Wellington, is said to have spent his youth at Dangan. Richard Wellesley spent vast sums developing Dangan Castle during the 18th century but unfortunately it was burned down in 1809.

Summerhill

Meath boasts two man-made waterways, one working and one defunct. The Royal Canal, which links Dublin to the river Shannon at Clondra in Longford, carves its way across the south-western corner of Meath, often accompanying the railway which led to its demise. The canal was completed in 1817, a major feat of 19th century engineering, exemplified by the beautiful aqueduct which carries the canal over the Boyne near Longwood. At places like Enfield there is access to the canal towpath, which affords walkers the opportunity to savour the peace and natural delights of the Meath countryside.

The Boyne Canal, linking Navan to Drogheda, was built between 1750 and 1800 to service the business and industrial needs of the area, since the Boyne was not navigable because of its many weirs. It was another wonderful feat of engineering, featuring some twenty locks and exquisite hump-backed bridges. Interestingly, the canal switches from one side of the river to the other as the landscape demands. It seems that when this happened, the horse that pulled the barge was taken on board and transported to the other side. How the poor animal must have enjoyed that brief respite!

The canal must initially have proved a boon to the many flour-millers of Navan and to the great Jebb mill at Slane, giving them direct access to the port of Drogheda from which their product was exported to England and beyond. As with the Royal Canal, the coming of the railway spelt the beginning of the end for the Boyne Canal and it was abandoned in 1923. Towards the end of the 19th century an enterprising tour operator ran Boyne cruises with the steam barge *SS Ros na Riogh* from Oldbridge near Drogheda to Beauparc. The tourist could stop off at Slane for lunch in the Boyneville Hotel (the former millhouse) and take a carriage to Newgrange, or continue on to Beauparc. From here he could take a train back to Drogheda in the afternoon. What a perfect day out – savouring all the delights of the Boyne valley at a graceful 19th century pace!

Today the Boyne Canal is in the care of An Taisce, the Irish National Trust. You can no longer take a barge but you can enjoy the Boyne Way, a delightful walk that follows the course of the canal. Beginning at the Ramparts at Athlumney in Navan, the Boyne Way takes the walker through woodland, past ruined castles like Dunmoe and into the very heart of the Royal County. Over the little bridges and past the decaying locks, you are lost in another world.

Waterways

The county of Meath is for the most part flat and lush pastureland, but in its north-east corner is a ridge of hills which entomb many of the secrets of its prehistoric past. At 911 ft, Loughcrew is Meath's highest point and clustered on three flat-topped hills are some thirty passage tombs. These tombs date from the Stone Age nearly five thousand years ago and it seems they were not just set aside for the dead. Our ancestors visited them for various ceremonial purposes. A passage tomb comprises a roofed passage and chamber, covered by a circular cairn of stones with a ring of kerbstones around each cairn. Inside, the chambers vary in design from cruciform to stall. In these recesses were placed the cremated human bones together with articles (hairpins, beads) that may have been worn by the dead. Folklore tells that the cairns were three piles of stones dropped from the apron of a hag as she flew over the hills. Hence the name *Sliabh na Caillighe* – 'the Hag's Hill'. A huge stone embedded in one of the cairns is known as the 'Hag's Chair'. Exploration of the cairns has brought evidence that the tombs were re-used during the Iron Age (600 BC – 500 AD). There is open access to Loughcrew and keys to the tomb are available locally. Bring a torch!

In medieval times Anglo-Norman settlements were developed around Loughcrew. The Plunkett family were granted a large tract of land. Oliver Plunkett, Archbishop of Armagh, was born in Loughcrew House. He was martyred for his faith in London in 1681 and in 1975 he was canonised. His skull can be seen in a shrine in St. Peter's Church, Drogheda. The Plunkett family were succeeded by the Napers in the 1650s. They remodelled the estate and in the eighteenth century Oldcastle was founded as a new village centre for the estate. Loughcrew House no longer stands but the walled garden remains together with a beautiful avenue of yew trees. There is also the ruin of the Plunkett family church. Nearby is a grassy mound which was once a 12th century Norman motte. To the south-east is Creeve Lough, which features a crannóg, a man-made island to which our ancestors retreated in time of attack.

In recent times Loughcrew Gardens have been the setting for open-air opera performances. Down the road lives Peter Fallon, an eminent poet, publisher and sometime farmer. His Gallery Press is a distinguished continuing outlet for his own work and that of many modern Irish poets and playwrights.

I warm to winter work, its rituals
and routines, and find - indoors
and out – a deal of pleasure, alone
or going out to work with neighbours,
a meitheal still. All I approve persists,
is here, at home. I think it exquisite
to stand in the yard, my feet on the ground
in cowshit and horseshit and sheepshit.

from *Winter Work* by Peter Fallon, News of the World
(Selected and New Poems), The Gallery Press, 1998

Loughcrew

About halfway between Kells and Navan the river Blackwater alters its south-easterly course to flow south, then east and north in the shape of a large U-bend. This bend contains the townland of Teltown (in Irish, *Tailtiú*), one of the most important ritual landscapes in Ireland. The Annals tell us that,

'In the reign of Lugh Lámhfhada, the Fair of
Tailteann was established in commemoration and
in remembrance of his foster-mother Tailtiú…'

The Fair would be held on the first day of August or Lughnasa (Lugh's Fair), to mark the beginning of the harvest season. During Tailtiú's reign as queen, the country enjoyed great prosperity and peace. *'Dew fell instead of rain and each year was fruitful.'* (A sort of prehistoric Celtic Tiger era…). She had the whole landscape cleared into a fertile plain where she would be buried. Various man-made features, such as earthworks, roadways and lakes were developed. The most noticeable features surviving today are two flat-topped circular mounds – Rath Dhú (the Black Fort) and Rath Airthir (the Eastern Fort), now overgrown – part of ancient roadway and two sloping mounds known locally as 'the Knockauns'.

The Fair of Tailteann featured various sports and pastimes – running, boxing, wrestling and other feats of strength and agility. There were horse-races and chariot-races, shows and plays.

Base of the High Cross,
Cill Tailteann

It was the High King's duty to attend but when Christianity came, the Fair had to have the approval of Church authorities. They cancelled it in 811 AD when *'neither horse nor chariot'* attended. The marauding Danes also caused the Fair some bother. The ancient church site of Donaghpatrick (Patrick's church) suggests that St. Patrick came this way. There are remains of ancient tombs near the modern church. Further afield, in the centre of the U-bend, are the remains of a medieval church.

The Fair of Tailteann continued until 1168 when the last High King of Ireland, Rory O'Connor, convened the final royal assembly there. Thereafter the Fair reverted to an annual Lughnasa festival. In the 1920s the Tailteann Games were revived for a period in Croke Park – a sort of homespun Olympic Games.

Tailtiú and her fair are still commemorated in the home of Gaelic Games in Meath – Páirc Tailteann in Navan.

Teltown

Kells is one of Ireland's oldest towns. Originally a settlement on the Blackwater River in prehistoric times, Columban monks came here from Iona in 804 AD following Viking attacks on the Scottish island. The relics of St. Colmcille were transferred to Kells in 877. The monastery flourished until about 1200 and its treasures included the famed *Book of Kells.* The Vikings continued to attack – three times in the 10th century alone – and the settlement was also raided by Irish chieftains, but the town still features outstanding treasures from monastic times. Three ornate 9th century crosses stand in the local churchyard, their carvings depicting scenes from the Bible. Near the entrance to the church grounds is the 90 ft round tower, built in the 11th century. The annals recall that Murchadh, king of Tara was murdered in the bell-tower in 1077. Nearby is St. Colmcille's House, a well-preserved oratory from the 11th century. It consisted of two storeys, the oratory above and possibly a scriptorium below, where some of the work on the *Book of Kells* might have been done. Another cross, the highly-ornate Market Cross, originally stood in the centre of the town. Over the centuries it suffered the vicissitudes of wars, weather and more recently articulated lorries! It is said that the grooves at its base were made by English soldiers sharpening their swords on the stone.

A major synod of the Irish church was held in Kells in 1152. At this synod the dioceses into which the Irish church is divided were established. In medieval times a Norman town and market were developed and it became known as Kenlis.

In recent centuries Kells developed as a market town, sited on the old coach road from Dublin to the north-west. It had a rail service from 1853 to 1958. In the late 17th century the Taylour family were given extensive lands in the Kells area. The Taylours subsequently became Marquesses of Headfort and in the 1760s Sir Thomas Taylour built Headfort House to the design of Dublin architect George Semple. After its completion he invited the renowned Scottish architect Robert Adam to design the interior of the house. Among his grandest designs is the Eating Parlour, with double-height ceiling and decorative plasterwork. In the 18th century Kells was developed as an estate town and part of that legacy is the courthouse (now a heritage centre) and an imposing row of Georgian houses at Headfort Place. Headfort House is now a boys' school and part of the estate is now the popular Headfort Golf club. A few miles beyond Kells off the Virginia road is another Headfort legacy – the Tower of Lloyd, an 18th century 'folly' built by the Marquis – although there are some who will insist that this 'lighthouse' was built by a man called Lloyd to enable his invalid mother to see the sea!

Market Cross, Kells

Kells

The *Book of Kells* is one of the most beautiful and most precious works of art from the Christian era. It comprises the four gospels written in Latin and illuminated by the monks of St. Colmcille around the year 800 AD. There is some debate as to whether it was written in Kells or in Iona, an island off the west coast of Scotland, where Colmcille lived in exile from 563 to his death in 597 AD. About two hundred years later, Iona was invaded by the Norsemen. The then abbot escaped to Kells where he founded a Columban monastery. A part of that monastery would have been the scriptorium, where the scribe-monks wrote, decorated and bound beautiful books made of vellum or calf-skin. It was painstaking work, full of the most intricate patterns and designs.

The *Book of Kells* or the 'Great Gospel of Colmcille' as it was once known, comprises 680 pages – 340 vellum leaves written and decorated on both sides. It is estimated that 150 calves would have been needed to supply that much vellum. The skin had to be steeped, scraped and stretched to produce good quality vellum. The scribes used goose-quills and made ink from the juices of plants and roots. The amazing rich colours used in the illustrations remain a mystery to modern science as to their origin. There

are full-page portraits of Christ and the evangelists Matthew and John and a number of full-page scenes from the life of Christ. Different styles appear and it is likely that a number of artists worked on the project, overseen by a 'master-mind'.

A work of art:
The Book of Kells

Sometimes the scribes added their own comments on the margins, for example, *'My only friend is God: I have no drinking-cup or goblet but my shoe'*. Being a scribe was a lonely, difficult task, undertaken in silence, but such was the artistry and dedication of these men that, twelve hundred years later, we can only gaze in awe at the clarity and beauty of their work.

In 1006 AD the *Annals of Ulster* recorded that *'the great gospel of Colmcille was stolen by night from the western sacristy of the great stone church of Cenennus (Kells)'*. Fortunately it was recovered a few months later but its gold cover and some end leaves were missing. The book was more carefully protected from then onwards and it survived in the church of Kells until the arrival of Cromwell in 1654 made the church authorities fearful for its safety. In 1661 Bishop Henry Jones of Meath placed it in the library of Trinity College Dublin together with another treasure, *The Book of Durrow*.

Today the *Book of Kells* is carefully preserved in the Treasury of Trinity College Library. Thousands of visitors come to view this great national treasure and can only marvel at the incredible artistry of those gifted men who combined to produce this beautiful book twelve hundred years ago in the most primitive conditions – working silently in damp, cold stone cells to honour God and their founder, Colmcille.

The Book of Kells

The Anglo-Normans settled at this river-crossing in 1180 and fortified the settlement with a wall. Athboy thus became an outpost on the fringe of the Pale – the lowland region surrounding Dublin that was under English rule in medieval times. A Carmelite monastery existed here between the 13th and 16th centuries. The de Verdon family built Rathmore Castle in the 13th century. It later passed through marriage to the Plunkett family, a name that became increasingly associated with many estates in Meath. Because of its location, Athboy suffered many incursions over the centuries. In the rebellion of 1641 Owen Roe O'Neill laid siege to the town a number of times. Oliver Cromwell's troops attacked it eight years later and, it is claimed, murdered twelve members of the Plunkett family. If wars were not enough, Athboy was devastated by the Great Drought and Plague of 1574 and again by cholera in the 19th century. Rathmore Castle fell into the hands of John Bligh, the Earl of Darnley, early in the 18th century and for the next two centuries the town and its surroundings were owned by the Darnleys until, following the Wyndham Land Act, the 7th Earl sold the town in 110 lots in 1909.

Outside the Catholic Church in Athboy stands a statue commemorating Athboy's best-known son, Eugene O'Growney, one of the prime movers of the Irish Language Revival Movement in the late 19th century. Eugene O'Growney was born in Ballyfallon, Athboy in 1863. When he was a teenager, a friend gave

Statue of Eugene O'Growney

him a rare Irish prayer-book. Around the same time he heard a local horse-trainer speak Irish, a rarity in those times. Both those events kindled a great interest in the Irish language in the young lad. In 1889 he entered the priesthood. He became Professor of Irish in Maynooth College and continued to study the language and to write about it. He compiled *Simple Lessons,* a basic Irish grammar which was widely used. His health began to fail and despite a move to sunnier climes in Los Angeles he died there in 1894. He is buried in Maynooth. Despite his short life he did much to help re-kindle a love for his native tongue.

Not far from the Athboy-Navan road is the Hill of Ward. This was reputedly the palace of Tlachtga (a pagan sorceress) two thousand years ago. Here at the beginning of November every three years, people assembled for the pagan festival of Samhain, which marked the beginning of winter. In 1167 Roderic O'Connor summoned a great assembly of clergy and chieftains – 'the power and patriotism of the day' – to the Hill of Ward to make and adopt laws and agreements.

Athboy today is a busy little town whose population has grown – in keeping with many other Meath towns – through becoming a dormitory town for Dublin. One of its most successful businesses is McElhinney's Fashion Emporium to which customers flock from the Pale and far beyond!

Athboy

Colonisation is a dark word in Irish history but an experiment in self-colonisation in Co. Meath has offered a somewhat brighter chapter. In 1935 the de Valera-led government came up with the idea of moving families from impoverished Gaeltacht (Irish speaking) areas in Connemara on the Western seaboard to the fertile plains of Meath. This would have the double objective of easing congestion in the west and promoting the native language in the east.

Estates in the Rath Cairn area, a few miles from Athboy, were taken over by the Land Commission and parcelled into holdings of twenty-two acres. Twenty-seven families moved from Connemara. Most had never travelled that far east before. To them, the rich plains of Meath looked like 'Tír na nÓg' in comparison to the rocky fields of Connemara in which they had struggled to survive previously. As one of the colonists put it *any place but the portach (bog) would have been welcome'.*

Each family was given a horse, a cow, other farm animals and farm equipment as well as a new house to settle into. There were isolated incidents of resentment from a few locals but generally the new arrivals were made to feel welcome. The parish priest of Athboy organised a welcoming concert. An anecdote of the time illustrates how the newcomers had brought their own customs with them. A young curate was baffled on being told in the confessional by a Connemara man that he had made poitín. Unsure of what penance he should impose for this new offence, he asked the parish priest what he should give the offender. "Arra", said the priest, "Give him a pound a bottle!"

Two of the original families left after a short while. They missed the portach too much. The rest settled in well but the times were harsh economically, and many had to emigrate in search of work. In 1974 Comharchumann Rath Cairn (a co-operative) was set up to help the two hundred or so who were still living in the tiny gaeltacht. Rath Cairn has survived as a social experiment and, approaching its 75th anniversary, it can be deemed a success. The Irish-speaking community flourishes with its own schools, music and drama festivals and Irish language courses. *Go maire siad an céad!*

Rath Cairn

For most people who live outside the county, Meath is synonymous with rich grasslands stocked with prime beef and dairy cattle, but the south-western corner of the county has extensive boglands, part of the Great Bog of Allen which stretches across Ireland's Central Plain. The village of Ballivor where I grew up stands on the fringe of that bogland and for generations the bog was an important part of the village's economic and social life.

Every year families would cut and 'save' their own turf from a rented piece of bogland, a turf-bank. This assured them of cheap fuel for the cold winter months. My father, the local garda sergeant, was no exception to this practice and each year we, his children, would be pressed into service to help save the turf. The turf-bank had first to be cleared of heather and scrub until the peat was exposed. The turf was then cut by hand with a double-sided spade called a slane, which sliced into the peat and cut sods of about one foot in length. Wielding the slane was a deft piece of artistry, involving a stab with the foot, a twist of the handle and a smooth toss of the sod in one easy action. It looked easy to do but it required strength and skill. Another man caught the glistening wet sods and heaped them on a special bog-barrow. A third man would wheel the barrow away from the bank and dump the load on high heathery ground. Our task as children was to spread the sods on the heather to expose them to drying sun and wind. It was relentless work. The barrow-loads kept

Working on the bog

coming and there was little rest from the back-bending work. We longed for the welcome break when we could sit and wolf down sandwiches and slake our thirst with the sweetest of tea, brewed there on the bog, while the men talked of politics and football. On another day we would return to 'foot' the turf – build it into little towers to enable the wind to dry it further. Later we would stack it in heaps and in about a month or so we would load it onto a lorry and ride home triumphantly with the winter fuel. The turf was saved.

During the war years, squads of soldiers were encamped on Ballivor Bog, cutting and saving turf to supply essential services in Dublin. In 1946 Bord na Móna (the Turf Board) moved in with giant turf-cutting machines called 'baggers' which harvested the peat commercially. A railway was laid across the bog to transport both turf and workmen. Ballivor had an industry. The days of hand-cut turf were numbered.

Recently, the bog brought worldwide attention to Ballivor when it gave up Cloneycavan Man, the well preserved remains (complete with hair-gel!) of a local who had died violently some 2,000 years ago.

Ballivor and Bogland

The sporting fields of Meath have a long history, dating back to the Fair of Tailteann in prehistoric times. Gaelic games and horse racing dominate, but Meath is a sporting county. A century-old soccer tradition flourishes in the modern Meath and District League. Rugby is strong in urban centres such as Navan and Ashbourne. Golf addicts have long-established parkland courses like Royal Tara, Headfort and Trim, a links course at Laytown-Bettystown and a proliferation of new courses in recent times. Athletics, cycling and handball have brought distinction to the Royal County but in terms of participation and often fanatical support, Gaelic games lead the way.

Meath clubs featured in the difficult early years of the Gaelic Athletic Association. Among them were the intriguingly-named Kells Campaigners and the North Meath Petitioners, but the club with the proudest history is undoubtedly Navan O'Mahonys, who were kingpins in the 1950s. At intercounty level Meath had to wait until 1949 for All-Ireland Senior Football success. Legendary names such as Paddy 'Hands' O'Brien, Paddy 'Stonewall' Dixon, Frankie Byrne, Brian Smyth and Peter 'the Man in the Cap' McDermott live on in the folk memory. The core of that team took another title in 1954 and there followed a long wait until 1967 when glory came again. Following this success Meath made a pioneering trip to Australia, the first step in the evolution of the modern 'International Rules' series. The arrival of Sean Boylan eventually ended a long famine in 1987 and during

"Come on the Royal!"

Boylan's long reign further glory came in 1988, 1996 and 1999. The most memorable year of all was 1991 when Meath and arch-rivals Dublin fought an amazing four-match saga. After five hours and forty minutes Meath were victorious by a single point, a victory fashioned by the greatest goal ever scored in Croke Park (the writer is clearly biased) – an eleven-man move finished by the most unlikely scorer, defender Kevin Foley!

Hurling has always been the 'Cinderella' of Gaelic games in Meath, being mainly restricted to loyal outposts like Trim, Dunboyne, Kildalkey, Killyon and Kilmessan, home of the legendary dual-player Tony Donnelly. Success at national level has been restricted to junior titles but hurling men would claim that Meath's greatest day was in 1929 when the minor hurlers beat the mighty Kilkenny!

The lush plains of Meath have long been devoted to a passionate interest in horse racing. Bellewstown Races have been in existence since 1726 and the Irish Grand National has been run at Fairyhouse since 1870. Navan is the other great popular venue and there is the unique once-a-year event on Laytown Strand.

For over one hundred and ten years sport in Meath has been faithfully chronicled by – of course – the *Meath Chronicle* newspaper.

Football and Racing

The Salmon of Knowledge

It was said that whoever tasted of the Salmon of Knowledge when it was caught in the Boyne would have the gift of knowledge. After years of pursuit, the wise man Fionnegas caught the fish. The salmon had to be cooked carefully over a spit. When the fire died, Fionnegas went in search of wood, leaving a young student of his in charge. If the fish was burned, the gift would be lost. A blister arose on the skin of the salmon and, mindful of the old man's warning, the boy pressed his thumb on the blister. He burned his thumb and instinctively put it in his mouth to ease the pain. Inadvertently he acquired the gift of knowledge. When the old man returned, he knew that his lifelong dream was lost to the innocent youth. The boy was Fionn Mac Cumhaill, who grew up to be the great warrior leader of the Fianna.

The Burial of King Cormac

Before he died, the High King Cormac MacAirt left instructions that he was to be buried at Rosnaree and not at the traditional resting place of Kings, Brugh na Bóinne, *'for he did not worship the same God as any of those at Brugh'*. Upon his death, his servants went against his wishes and attempted to bury him at Brugh. Each time they tried, *'the Boyne swelled up thrice, so that they could not cross'*. They recognised they were violating the king's wishes *'and they afterwards dug his grave at Rosnaree as he had ordered'*.

The Irish Crown Jewels

When King George IV of England came to Slane Castle in 1821 to see his mistress Lady Conyngham, the naughty fellow gave her jewellery that had been worn by his queen, Charlotte. On the king's death, Lady Conyngham returned the jewellery to Dublin Castle where the valuable diamonds, rubies and emeralds were reworked into insignia for the Illustrious Order of St. Patrick and they became known as the Irish Crown Jewels. In 1907, a few days before the visit of King Edward VII, the Crown Jewels disappeared. A century later, the search goes on.

The Foxes of Gormanstown

In the 14th century Gormanstown Castle was taken over from the original Gormans by the Preston family who came from Preston in Lancashire. The Preston coat of arms features the figure of a fox. Legend has it that when the head of the house dies, and for some days before, foxes leave all the neighbouring coverts and collect at the door of the castle. In 1911 Lady Gormanston reported that, on the death of her husband, the foxes came to the castle "barking and making many uncanny and creepy noises…"

Legends, Myths and Mysteries

The Story of Meath

They came slowly over a period of time in small groups, maybe just one family, daring to trust their fragile boats to wind and wave on the Irish Sea. They were not the first people in Ireland but these people who set foot on our shores about six thousand years ago were different. Unlike their predecessors who were hunters and at the mercy of nature, these newcomers had learned to control their environment. They could tame and breed animals. They had learned how to scatter seeds and cultivate grain. Land was growing scarce across Europe as the human population increased. And so they came, these revolutionaries, mainly to our north-eastern shores since that was the shortest crossing, but also to river estuaries further south – to the Boyne estuary, for instance. The fishing was good here, but as they made their way inland and slowly cleared woodland and scrub, the newcomers found that the soil was rich and suited to their needs. It was tough and laborious work. They had only stone axes to work with, but they persisted and gradually cleared more and more tracts of land. But unlike the hunters who had to move on in search of food, the newcomers knew how to till the soil, grow crops and keep animals for their meat and milk and hides. They could settle in a place. More of them came and the newcomers worked their way further and further into the Boyne valley. The first Meath farmers had arrived.

We know little enough about these first farmers – how they communicated, what their houses were like. They would have lived in isolation from each other, raising their animals and growing corn. They would have been prosperous on the fertile soil they inhabited. We know more about them in death than in life. They built the great stone monuments at Newgrange, Knowth, Dowth and Loughcrew to the memory of the dead and probably for subsequent religious events. Even with the most primitive of stone tools they carved amazing patterns on the huge stones in those passage-tombs. The sun played a major role in their lives, as we know from the alignment of the Newgrange tomb.

Civilisation was on the march. About a thousand years after the coming of the farmers, the first metal-workers reached our shores. They knew about smelting and mixing ores to produce bronze and they now had bronze tools and weapons to make great cauldrons and pots. They found gold and fashioned beautiful artefacts. The migrations from Europe were not yet over; about 600 BC a new wave of warrior-invaders came west from central Europe. They probably arrived in Ireland both in the north – from Scotland – and in the south – from France and Spain. They comprised different tribes who were linked by a common language and similar appearance and dress. They had a new weapon – iron. They were the Celts. One tribe who came from Gaul (France) were known as the Brigantes and settled in Magh Breagha – roughly the modern counties of Meath and Dublin. The Celts were a pagan people who had their own rituals and whose year began at Samhain (November 1st). This festival together with two others – Bealtaine (May 1st) and Lughnasa (August 1st) – were the high points of the Celtic year. The Celts eventually formed themselves into about 150 small kingdoms called tuatha. Gradually these tuatha coalesced into four large kingdoms or provinces – Ulster, Leinster, Munster and Connacht.

Sometime in the second century AD, a king named Tuathal Teachtmar created a fifth province – Meath – by taking portions or 'necks' from the other four provinces. Some historians derive the name from *meidhe,* a neck. There were four great royal palaces in the new province – Tara, Tailtiú or Teltown on the Blackwater, Tlachtga or the Hill of Ward near Athboy and Uisneach in modern Westmeath. The province of Meath stretched from the Shannon to the sea – roughly the equivalent of the modern diocese of Meath.

The Celts were a rural society. They lived on isolated farms and often built their houses and farm buildings within raths (forts) on high ground. Their wealth was primarily their cattle and this wealth was often the cause of squabbles between kingdoms, for example Táin Bó Cuailgne, the great cattle raid carried out by the men of Connacht into Ulster. Another influential 'wave' washed into this rural society from Europe in the fifth century. This wasn't an invasion as such but its influence would echo through the centuries right down to our own times. It was the arrival of Christianity.

CHRISTIANITY

Patrick, the slave-boy who returned to Ireland in response to visions he had of the Irish people calling him back as a missionary, eventually reached these shores in 432 AD. He travelled about the midlands, north and west particularly, preaching, converting and organising the early church. A year after his arrival he lit the Easter fire at Slane, thus incurring the wrath of King Laoghaire who was about to light his own fire at Tara as part of a pagan festival. A confrontation ensued and the King was so impressed by the missionary that he allowed him to continue preaching. Over the next few centuries monastic settlements proliferated all over Ireland. Meath had several notable centres of learning and prayer. St. Finnian established his 'university' at Clonard. Columban monks exiled from Iona settled in Kells and produced one of the great artistic treasures, the *Book of Kells.* St. Loman founded a monastery at a ford on the Boyne called Trim. On the banks of the river Nanny, the monk Cianán, who was a stonemason, reputedly built the first stone church in Ireland and attracted a large community to settle there. These centres of prayer, farmwork and learning became busy settlements and grew into early towns.

On the civil side, all was not serenity and prayer, however. There were ongoing disputes and invasions among the provincial kings. In 481 AD the Uí Néill dynasty extended their power into Meath with a decisive victory at the Battle of Ocha, about four miles north-west of Navan. They proclaimed themselves kings of all Ireland but this was far from the truth. There were continuing invasions from Leinster and Connacht. The great roads led to Tara but Tara did not always control them. In truth there was little enough travel. People lived in isolation within raths or as in Lagore, near Dunshaughlin, in crannógs or lake-dwellings, to defend themselves against cattle-raiders. There was a greater threat

on the way however, not from neighbouring kings but from across the northern seas. The Vikings were coming.

The Vikings

Driven by increasing population in their homeland of Scandinavia and Denmark and by an adventurous seafaring and trading spirit, the Vikings first made land in 795 AD at Lambay Island off the Dublin coast. Others soon followed in great fleets of massive open longboats. By 837 AD they were said to have sixty ships on the Boyne alone. Each ship would carry up to sixty men and such was the ship's design they could navigate not only oceans but also rivers and lakes. This was bad news for Boyne country. The Vikings were fierce and merciless warriors who slaughtered and ransacked their way inland, terrorising homesteads and monasteries alike. Round towers were built at Donaghmore and Kells to watch out for their coming and to hide on their arrival. The Vikings' progress was relentless as there was no common defence against them. The Irish kings were often squabbling with each other and the Vikings often sided with one Irish kingdom against another. At times the Irish did combine, particularly against Turgesius who had *'assumed the sovereignty of all the foreigners in Ireland'* and in 845 AD Turgesius was killed in battle by Malachy, king of Meath. Ten years later Malachy invaded Munster in an attempt to enforce the authority of the Uí Néill over all of Ireland. A successor of his, Malachy II, inflicted a heavy defeat on the Dublin Vikings at Tara in 980 and went to attack and loot

Dublin itself. Malachy eventually had to cede kingship of Ireland to the rising power of Munster in the person of Brian Boru. Brian finally broke the power of the Vikings at the battle of Clontarf in 1014 AD. The pagan Vikings became Christians, intermarried with the Irish and settled as traders and merchants. They founded many Irish towns at trading ports, notably Dublin. From now on Dublin would be the political centre of Ireland. The power had swung away from Tara and the other royal palaces.

While the Norse invaders were now at peace, unrest continued among the provincial kingdoms of Ireland. The province of Meath suffered most, coming under constant attack from Connacht and Munster in the eleventh and twelfth centuries. After the death of Malachy II in 1022 Meath went into decline and became a pawn for other provinces to fight over. In 1055 the men of Connacht laid waste to Meath. In 1105 Donogh O'Melaghlin, the King of Meath, was driven out by Murtough O'Brien of Munster. Twenty years later Turlough O'Connor, King of Connacht, divided Meath into four portions but his great rival O'Lochlainn from Ulster invaded Meath in 1128 and *'burned Ath Troim and its churches'*. Rory O'Connor, son of Turlough, became the last High King of Ireland in 1166 but it would be a short reign. Another squabble between O'Rourke of Breifne and Diarmuid McMurrough of Leinster led the latter going abroad to seek help, an event which led to the next great chapter in Irish history.

Despite all this unrest, this same period (11-12th centuries) was also a time of great learning across Ireland. Scholars gathered story and tradition into great manuscripts. The Irish Church was also reformed after the ravages of the Norsemen and a major Synod was held in Kells in 1152. At this Synod Ireland was divided into four archbishoprics – Armagh, Dublin, Cashel and Tuam – and thirty-six dioceses were established. Progress was being made, but dark clouds were on the horizon.

THE COMING OF THE NORMANS

Dermot McMurrough's mission abroad was successful and in 1169 he joined with his new allies, the Normans, descendants of the earlier Viking raiders. They quickly overran Leinster under their leader Strongbow. Two years later King Henry II came over to Ireland to establish his lordship of the country. He gained the submission of the Irish kings, the Norman princes and the Church leaders and in a matter of six months he had gained control of much of the eastern half of the country. This control he consolidated by granting the lands of the Irish kings to Norman lords. He made one of his most loyal supporters, Hugh de Lacy, viceroy in his absence and granted him the whole kingdom of Meath, famously *for the service of fifty knights'* in war time. De Lacy proceeded to drive out the native rulers and install his own barons. He carved Meath into twelve baronies – Duleek, Slane, Navan, Kells, Fore, Deece, Morgallion, Lune, Dunboyne, Ratoath, Skryne and Moyfenrath. Families such as de Feypo, Plunkett, Dalton, Nugent, Fleming and Nangle soon established themselves across Meath, building strong castles and employing the feudal system of control in their estates. The great castles at Trim and Dunsany were built at strategic locations. Settlements at Trim, Athboy and Navan were walled for defensive purposes. Hugh de Lacy took Rose the daughter of Rory O'Connor as his second wife – probably as much a 'strategic' move as anything else! While the Gaelic princes in the west and south continued to resist the Norman conquest in the thirteenth century, the kingdom of de Lacy was in relative peace. The Normans introduced a system of centralised government, a court system and coinage. (Trim would have a Royal Mint in the 15th century.) They also introduced the notion of shires or counties and in 1205 King John, successor to Henry II, constituted Meath as *'a shire of the English Pale'*.

A shire was controlled by a sheriff who collected revenue, presided over courts and administered justice. As well as the county of Meath there was also the 'liberty of Trim' under the control of Roger de Mortimer. The liberty was a similar form of administration to the shire, and the fact that there was a liberty of Trim underlines the importance of that town as a centre of administration in the 14th century. The Normans were actually few in number and gradually assimilated the language and customs of the Irish, becoming 'more Irish than the Irish themselves'. They were not so much loyal to the English crown as anxious to hold their own estates.

When Edward Bruce and his force of six thousand Scottish troops invaded Ireland in 1315, many Norman Irish joined with them when they marched into Meath. Despite initial success in his efforts to prevent the king of England using Ireland as a source of men and supplies in his Scottish campaign, Edward Bruce and his army were ultimately routed at the Battle of Faughart, near Dundalk in 1318. They were beaten by a colonial army of the gentry and militia of Meath and nearby towns such as Drogheda.

<u>WITHIN THE PALE</u>

The English colony in Ireland was now reduced to 'the Pale' which included the county of Meath, just about. The Pale in medieval times was subjected to regular raids by such as the O'Connors of Offaly and the O'Reillys of Breifne. In 1435 the Irish council complained to King Richard II,

> *'that there is not left in the nether parts of the counties of Dublin, Meath, Louth and Kildare, out of the subjection of the said enemies and rebels scarcely thirty miles in length and twenty miles in breadth, thereas a man may surely ride or go in the said counties to answer the king's writ and do his commandments…'*

In 1539 the princes of the North, O'Neill and O'Donnell, plundered as far south as Tara. They were eventually routed but their devastation of Meath led to the walling of Navan. By this time, the Tudors were on the throne of England and

Henry VIII had established himself as Head of the Church in England and Ireland. Part of his policy was to dissolve the monasteries and in the space of five years (1536-41) the monasteries at Trim, Navan, Bective and Duleek had been surrendered. The monasteries had not just been spiritual centres. They were also the hospitals, schools and inns of the country and their closure was a great loss to the people, particularly within the Pale. Henry VIII was declared King of Ireland in 1541, the first monarch to bear this title. In 1543 an Act of Parliament created the new counties of East and West Meath, with Trim and Mullingar being the respective administrative capitals. Successive Tudor monarchs continued Henry's policy of the Anglicisation of Ireland and it was Elizabeth I who finally brought *that rude and barbarous nation to civility*. The defeat of O'Neill and O'Donnell at Kinsale in 1601 marked the end of the old Irish order.

REBELLION AND PLANTATION

The middle part of the 17th century was a time of great turmoil in both Ireland and England. This turmoil in turn led to great changes in the ownership of land in Ireland. A civil war raged in England between king and parliament. Sensing that the time was right, dispossessed landowners in Ulster rebelled and the rebellion spread countrywide. The rebels sided with royalists in England. The noblemen of Meath met at Tara and defeated the English troops at the Battle of Julianstown. Soon the rebels had taken Trim, Navan, Kells and Athboy. In 1642 Sir Charles Coote, who was Governor

of Dublin and a leader of the English force, was shot dead in Trim. Leading the rebels were Owen Roe O'Neill in Ulster and Thomas Preston of the Gormanstown family in Leinster. The rebels, often riven by divisions (not an uncommon story in Ireland), had mixed fortunes. O'Neill won notable victories at Portlester (near Ballivor) in 1643 and at Benburb in Co. Tyrone in 1646 but Preston was defeated at Dungan's Hill near Trim in 1647. In 1649, however, Charles I was executed in England and Oliver Cromwell took command of the Parliamentary army in Ireland. The end was nigh for the rebels. With an army of 12,000 soldiers, Cromwell wrought a trail of terror beginning in Drogheda. The garrison at Trim fled in panic. A Cromwellian force laid waste to Athboy where they are said to have murdered twelve members of the Plunkett family. Cromwell's progress was relentless and thorough and by 1653 the rebellion was totally quashed. Cromwell's financial backers, known as 'adventurers', had to be repaid, however. They would be repaid with Irish land. The rebels' lands would be confiscated and the landowners sent 'to hell or to Connacht'. Six and a half million acres were given to English planters. To find out how much land was available, a Civil Survey was carried out under Sir William Petty. This was a huge exercise, mapping every piece of land and every town. Kells, for example, was described thus,

'There being one castle, a church with a steeple, a tucke (woollen) mill and two corn mills, divers houses and

cabins, a stone quarry, a fishing weir and two waste mills. The walls of the said town being ruinate…'

Many of the adventurers did not take up their lands, preferring to sell them and return to England. There were 19,000 acres on offer in the Barony of Navan but only 865 acres were claimed. 8,000 acres were sold, one of the biggest purchasers being John Preston who bought the Ardsallagh estate. He later became MP for Meath and set up a school – Preston School – where the Navan Shopping Centre stands today. The school lasted until 1967.

Upon the restoration of King Charles II in England, many landowners sought to recover their properties and a Court of Claims was set up in 1662. One of the great aids to the study of history in recent times has been the number of local studies carried out by historians and enthusiasts. A case in point is *Charlesfort – the story of a Meath estate and its People, 1668-1968,* by Tony Coogan and Jack Gaughran. This is the story of the Manor of Martry, midway between Navan and Kells and I am grateful to the authors for the following insights.

The Darcy family were of Norman descent and had been granted the manor of Martry in the 14th century for their service to the king. Nicholas Darcy had taken part in the 1641 Rebellion and as a result his lands were confiscated. He appealed to the Court of Claims and had part of his lands restored to his grandson. He was in financial difficulties however and was forced to lease out the manor of Martry to a young lawyer who had an eye for a good property, Michael Tisdall. The lease documents give a fascinating insight into a fairly typical Meath estate of the time. On the manor were

- *ten messuages (houses and grounds)*
- *ten tofts (messuages with right of common)*
- *two windmills*
- *one hundred cottages*
- *a pigeonhouse*
- *twenty gardens*
- *five hundred acres of land*
- *two hundred acres of meadow*
- *one thousand acres of pasture*
- *fifty acres of woods*
- *fifty acres of heath*
- *one hundred acres of moor*

The above lands were let in part to tenant-farmers and cottiers and the Tisdall family remained in control of the Charlesfort estate (so-called after the house Charles Tisdall built on the land) for three hundred years. The Charlesfort story is a classical example of how land-ownership changed in 17th century Ireland. The majority of landowners were now Protestant and their estates brought them wealth. For their tenants, however, life was grim enough. They lived mainly on milk and milk products in primitive houses. Their farm equipment was very basic and roads, where they existed, were very poor. Apart from losing their lands, Catholics also had difficulty in the practice of their religion. Priests were persecuted or in exile. Oliver Plunkett from Loughcrew had gone to Rome to study for the priesthood. He eventually returned to Ireland in 1670 as Archbishop of Armagh and set about re-organising the Catholic church. He had to go into hiding himself for six months. He finally fell victim to a 'Popish plot' which supposedly was aimed at replacing Charles II by his Catholic brother, James. He was arrested and executed for treason in London in 1681.

EIGHTEENTH CENTURY IRELAND

James II did accede to the throne of England, which ultimately led to the 'War of the Two Kings' between himself and his son-in-law William of Orange. This culminated in James being routed at Oldbridge on the Boyne in 1690. For those who supported James, retribution was at hand. The Flemings of Slane had their estate confiscated. It came into the hands of the Conynghams who came from Mountcharles in Co. Donegal. They were a symbol of the Protestant ascendancy who dominated Irish life in the 18th century. Sir Launcelot Dowdall burned his castle at Athlumney rather than cede it to William and in common with thousands of his countrymen, fled to the continent.

A succession of penal laws was introduced early in the 18th century to exclude Catholics from political power. Many Catholic landlords – among them Lord Dunsany – joined the established church. By 1776 only five per cent of the land was in Catholic ownership. Land and the labour of its tenants constituted wealth. If we return to the Tisdall family in Tony Coogan's study of Charlesfort, we can get an insight into life in rural Meath in the 18th century. Much of the Tisdall estate was leased to tenant farmers for periods of 21 or 31 years. Some of these were relatively well-off, like Hugh Lowther who rented 150 acres. He in turn would sub-let his land. Thady Mucklevaney rented 2 and a half acres, on which he had a mud cabin and a potato garden. His lease would only be for one year. There was extreme poverty among the cottiers; the fortunate ones might get work on the estate.

The linen industry was important in Meath (exports of wool were forbidden) and Charles Tisdall had a flax mill for which in 1743 he ordered 20 spinning wheels, 4 reels, 2 looms and a bleaching pan. At about the same time he began building his new residence – Charlesfort – in the Palladian style. His account books tell of 49,000 slates bought in Ballyjamesduff, three thousand bog laths purchased, two hundred trees planted, bricks were burned by Yates the brickmaker, 79 feet of Ardbraccan stone was purchased for the kitchen hearth (the White Quarry in Ardbraccan provided limestone for many Dublin public buildings of the period), and a lake, a duck-pond and a tennis-court were built. Charles lived well. He had his clothes and wigs made in Dublin, paid £18 for a hogshead of claret, lost £97 at cards while in Trim attending the Assizes but won most of it back at the 'Goat's Whey' pub.

He paid £5/13/9 to attend the first performance of Handel's *Messiah* and took holidays in Paris and Italy. Meanwhile the cottiers and the many poor in the towns eked out a grim existence in their cold and smoky hovels … Worlds apart.

For all that, progress was being made in commerce and communication. The Dublin-Navan coach road was completed in 1729 and four years later it was extended to Kells and Nobber. This aided the expansion of the postal system. You could board the coach at Queen Street, Dublin on Tuesday, Thursday or Saturday at noon for a fare of seven shillings and sevenpence inside (or five and fivepence outside) and be in nice time for tea in Navan at 5.30 pm (I am aware that modern commuters could tell similar tales) – providing the highwayman didn't detain you and relieve you of your valuables at the Black Bull… From 1750 onwards you could travel at an even more leisurely pace from Navan to Drogheda on the newly-built Boyne Canal. Navan was a growing town with flax and flour-mills, a distillery and a weekly market in the town shambles. Navan Corporation owned 1200 acres of commons and its Mayor imposed tolls and taxes.

Inspired by the revolution in France, the United Irishmen sought liberty and equality in this country and rose in rebellion in 1798 with help from France. The rebellion was quickly quelled even though a few brave stands were made in Meath – in Dunboyne (subsequently reduced to ruins by the yeomen), Slane and finally at Tara where 500 croppies fell before the yeos under Lord Fingall. His kinsman, Bishop Patrick Plunkett preached against the *folly and guilt of rebellion*, blaming it on *'the credulity of the lower classes, the decay of Christian piety and the prevalence of the impious principles that are disturbing a great part of the Continent…'*

NINETEENTH CENTURY MEATH

Patrick Plunkett died in 1827. He had been parish priest of Navan and Bishop of Meath for almost half a century. He had witnessed penal times, rebellion and the Act of Union which had united the parliaments of Britain and Ireland. He had not lived to see Daniel O'Connell win emancipation for Catholics in 1829. O'Connell then set about winning repeal of the Act of Union. Part of his strategy of influencing public opinion was to organise 'monster' meetings. The greatest of these was held at Tara on August 15th, 1843 when hundreds of thousands turned up to the hear 'the Liberator'. It was an unhappy countryside at the time. There was much agrarian unrest, provoked by the transition from tillage to grazing, the consolidation of small farms, eviction over unpaid rents and poor potato harvests – an omen of things to come. Secret societies abounded. At Rushwee, near Slane, 7,000 people assembled in 1832 to protest against the collection of tithes.

On their travels through Ireland in 1842 Mr and Mrs Hall wrote of the huge contrasts that existed in Co. Meath;

'The county of Meath is the great grazing ground of Ireland and consists almost entirely of pastureland, vying in its external aspects with the richest of the English counties and perhaps surpassing any of them in fertility… Much of this apparently prosperous character is, however, hollow and unsubstantial; the large farmers are indeed wealthy, but of small farmers there are few or none; the policy of the 'graziers' has been for a long time to devote the produce of the soil to the raising of cattle and the clearing of estates in Meath has been proceeding at a very disastrous rate… The consequence is that the towns, into which the poor have been driven, are thronged with squalid countenances; starvation stalks at noon-day through their streets and perhaps in no part of the world could be found so much wretchedness huddled together into an equal space as the tourist may note in the single town of Navan… We entered some of these hovels and were shocked to find their condition wretched almost beyond conception and certainly beyond credibility. The scene appalled us the more because of the lovely and plentiful land we had previously passed through; the fat cattle feeding upon pastures so fresh and green; the huge stacks; the full barns, the comfortable houses…'

Just a few years later, to heap further misery on the poor, came the Great Famine. The north-west of Meath was the worst affected, but the entire county suffered. The workhouses in Navan, Trim, Kells and Dunshaughlin were severely overcrowded. In 1848 there were 931 inmates in the Kells workhouse which had been built for 500. The population of the county dropped by 43,000 between 1841 and 1851. That drop was roughly evenly split between death and emigration. In the spring of 1847, 200 poor from the parish of Ballivor were cleared out of the Darnley estate and given passage to America. In 1850 out of 4,000 orphan girls sent to Australia, 100 came from Meath. According to Bishop Nulty of Meath, nearly 30,000 homes were levelled in his diocese. Fr. Anthony Cogan, the historian of the diocese, wrote trenchantly of the landlords as 'the crowbar brigade'. He became champion of 'the defenceless poor' and in 1871 he addressed a 'monster meeting' of some 10,000 tenant-farmers at Mullagh in Co. Cavan. A year later he was dead at the age of 45. This remarkable man gave himself totally to the service of his people as priest, writer, defender, founder of the Catholic Young Men's Society in Navan and as dean of St. Finnian's Seminary in Navan (founded in 1802 by Bishop Plunkett and relocated to Mullingar in 1908). The struggle to break the landlords' power and win back the land for the tenants would continue until a series of Land Acts between 1870 and 1909 finally resolved the land problem.

A major positive development in the latter half of the 19th century was the coming of the railway. In 1850 the Drogheda-Navan line was opened and was later extended to Kells and Oldcastle. The extension passed through the Charlesfort estate, mentioned earlier, and a station was built at Ballybeg. In 1900, on the occasion of Queen Victoria's visit to Dublin, Major Tisdall of Charlesfort organised a trip from Ballybeg to Dublin for local schoolchildren. In 1862 the Dublin-Navan line was opened and was later extended to Kingscourt. The railways had a century of glory. Both lines were closed for passenger traffic by 1959.

In the 1860s the Fenian movement gathered pace in its determination to achieve independence from Britain by force. Ultimately their efforts ended in failure in 1867 but a prominent part in the development of the organisation was played by the poet and journalist from Dowth, John Boyle O'Reilly. The movement for Home Rule as a stepping stone to independence gained momentum with the emergence of a young Protestant landlord from Co. Wicklow. Charles Stewart Parnell was twenty-nine when he was elected MP for Meath in 1875. He spoke regularly at meetings in Market Square, Navan, on the question of land agitation and by 1882 he had emerged as the *uncrowned King of Ireland*. His star fell, however, when he was named co-respondent in a divorce case by the husband of Kitty O'Shea. The Home Rule Party was split in its support of Parnell. Support for him was strong in Meath. Pierce O'Mahony (who would give his name to the Navan Gaelic Football club), the MP for Meath, was a strong Parnellite and when the leader visited Navan in 1891 his supporters came to help him *in his hour of trial*. His former colleague Michael Davitt spoke against Parnell at the Fair Green in Navan and was attacked by a mob. Later that

year, however, Parnell took ill and died. In the 1892 election Davitt took on and beat O'Mahony in North Meath, while another anti-Parnellite, Patrick Fullam, won in South Meath. The century ended with both the great questions – Home Rule and Land Reform still unresolved.

INDEPENDENCE

With the passing of the Wyndham Act in 1903 the land question was finally resolved. On September 9th 1904, the *Meath Chronicle* reported that *'tenants of the estate of C. A. Tisdall (Charlesfort Estate) met with the agent at his residence in Martry and signed agreements to purchase their holdings...'* The Demesne Farm was retained by the Tisdalls until 1968 – the end of a 300 year era. The bell that once summoned the workers on the estate now calls worshippers to prayer on a Nigerian mission.

The Irish Volunteers finally struck for freedom on Easter Monday 1916 but five days later Pearse surrendered. The only action that had taken place outside of Dublin was in Ashbourne where Thomas Ashe led a successful attack on the RIC Initial reaction to the rebellion was far from supportive. Navan Urban District Council *deplored the recent disturbance in Dublin*. Opinions changed when the leaders were executed. Meanwhile a horrific war raged on the continent of Europe and among the 49,000 Irish citizens that died in action with the British forces was a young poet from Slane, Francis Ledwidge. In the general election of 1918 Sinn

Féin took 73 of the 105 Irish Seats and in January 1919 they convened as the first Dáil Eireann and issued a Declaration of Independence. Representing Meath were two notable nationalists, Liam Mellowes and Eamon Duggan, who would become one of the signatories of the 1921 Treaty. The War of Independence was led in Meath by General Sean Boylan. On Halloween 1919 attacks were carried out on Navan and Ballivor barracks. In the latter case a constable was shot dead. There were many raids on big houses and rural barracks. Meath Volunteers suffered their first loss when Seamus Cogan was shot dead in Oldcastle. A successful raid on Trim barracks in 1920 was followed by bitter reprisals from the Black and Tans. Langford House in Summerhill was burned down because it was suspected to be a base for the Tans. Four days later the Tans burned and looted the village of Robinstown. Finally a truce was declared in July 1921.

The signing of the Treaty only set brother against brother in a bloody Civil War. Sean Boylan was pro-Treaty and took the majority of the Meath Volunteers with him. On the anti-Treaty side Mick Hilliard led the IRA forces. A fierce gun-battle at Dunderry left a man dead on either side. There were further attacks on Garda Barracks and train stations but gradually the anti-Treaty side was weakened. Liam Mellowes was executed in December 1922. A week later Mick Hilliard was arrested and in May 1923 the Civil War ended. A general election in August gave Cumann na nGael a majority. In Meath the three seats went to Cumann na nGael, Labour

and the Farmers' Party. With its formation in 1932, Fianna Fáil became the ruling party nationally and in Meath it usually held two out of three or three out of five seats in subsequent elections. When Fianna Fáil withheld land annuities from Britain in 1932, a six-year 'economic war' ensued which caused particular hardship for Meath cattle-farmers. Mick Hilliard carved out a thirty-year career in Dáil Eireann as a Fianna Fáil TD. Jimmy Tully flew the Labour flag for almost three decades. John Bruton emerged as a Fine Gael TD in 1973 and went on to lead the party and ultimately became the first Meath Taoiseach in 1994. In 1989 Mary Wallace became Meath's first woman TD. In the most recent election a burgeoning population caused the old Meath constituency to be split into Meath East and Meath West.

Postscript

What would Meath's first farmers of 6,000 years ago think of modern Meath? An impossible question. What of Hugh de Lacy who dotted the county with stone castles? Ah, he might say, the Pale is strong and growing! What of Thady Mucklevaney, the 18th century cottier or the wretches Mr and Mrs Hall came across in the hovels of 19th century Navan? A Meath they could never have imagined. The village of Ballivor that I grew up in, over a mere half-century ago, is totally changed in both its topography and demography. It is now a dormitory town for Dublin with a population greatly expanded in both numbers and diversity. The Pale is indeed strong and growing. Now we call it Greater Dublin.

The population of Meath is now 163,000 according to the 2006 census – an increase of over one-fifth in five years. Hamlets like Ratoath, Kildalkey and Enfield have seen increases of between half and two-thirds. This puts a strain on infrastructure. A new motorway is being built, despite severe protests over its route through the Tara-Skryne valley. It is hoped to restore the Dublin-Navan railway. Will that suffice? And what of the new population? Will it be readily assimilated into local communities? A more immediate and worrying consideration is the huge rise in unemployment in these 'new' towns as the post-tiger recession bites more deeply. The future is as always, uncertain, since it is yet to be shaped. Whatever about the future, Meath will always have its glorious and noble past. Up the Royal!

Sons of Meath

BEAUFORT, FRANCIS

Born in Navan in 1774, Francis was the son of the local rector who was a noted map-maker and a founder of the Royal Irish Academy. He was educated in Dublin, where he spent some time studying astronomy at Dunsink Observatory. He joined the British Navy and served in the Napoleonic Wars. He was seriously wounded in 1800 and was sent home to Navan to recover. He used this time to work on many experiments and inventions, among them Ireland's first telegraph line. Returning to sea, he became hydrographer to the British Navy, surveying and mapping the seas of the world. He is best known for inventing the Beaufort Scale of wind velocity, which we still use today. He died in 1857.

BOYLAN, GENERAL SEAN

Born in 1880. A member of the Irish Republican Brotherhood, he was arrested after the 1916 Rising and imprisoned in Britain where he became friendly with Michael Collins. Following his release in 1917 he became Brigadier of the Meath Brigade of the IRA. He was heavily involved in the War of Independence, notably in the burning of Trim RIC Barracks. He was badly injured in a munitions accident in 1919 but continued in active service, supporting the pro-Treaty side in the Civil War. A noted hurler in his youth, in his private life he developed a successful business as a herbalist, which he passed on to his son, Sean. Died 1971.

BOYLAN, SEAN

Born 1943. See under Dunboyne.

BROSNAN, PIERCE

Born 1953. Originally from Navan, this actor has had a distinguished career in film and television. He invariably plays the role of a smart, suave gentleman – experience which eventually led him to play James Bond in three Bond films in the 1990s.

BRUTON, JOHN

Born 1947. Politician, first elected as a Fine Gael TD for Meath in 1969. Minister for Finance in 1982 when his budget led to a Government defeat. Leader of Fine Gael from 1990 to 2001. Taoiseach of a Rainbow Coalition Government from 1994 to 1997. Currently EU Ambassador to Washington. His brother Richard is at present Fine Gael's Finance spokesman.

COGAN, ANTHONY

Born in Slane in 1826. Priest, scholar and historian. His great three-volume history of the Diocese of Meath was the first complete history of an Irish diocese. A gifted preacher and social reformer, he championed the cause of tenant farmers against landlord power. Founder of the Catholic Young Men's Society in Navan. The buildings he erected for the youth of the town stand as his memorial. Died 1872.

CORRIGAN, RICHARD

Born in Ballivor, 1964. Chef. He is the owner of award-winning restaurants in London and Dublin and is a regular presenter of food programmes on television.

COWLEY, JOHN

Actor who played the role of Tom Riordan in RTE television's long-running rural 'soap' *The Riordans.* Died 1998.

DONLON, SEAN

Diplomat, Former Irish ambassador to the USA.

DUNSANY, LORD EDWARD

See under The Plunkett Castles.

FALLON, PETER

See under Loughcrew.

FITZSIMONS, JIM

Politician, Fianna Fáil TD, 1977-87. Member of the European parliament for Leinster since 1984.

GILES, CAPTAIN PATRICK

Born in Longwood, 1901. Active in the War of Independence, he was imprisoned in 1921 and released just before the Treaty was signed. He joined the National Army, rising to the rank of captain. Entered politics and was a Fine Gael TD from 1937 until 1961. Died 1965.

GILSON, LAURENCE

Born in Oldcastle. Made his fortune in England and when he died in 1810 he left all his money for the erection of *'a schoolhouse on the green of Oldcastle'.* The Gilson Endowed

School provided primary and secondary education in Oldcastle for nigh on a century and a half.

HILLIARD, MICHAEL

Born 1902. Republican who led the IRA in Meath during the Civil War. Elected a Fianna Fáil TD for Meath in 1943 and served that constituency for thirty years, holding ministerial posts twice. Died 1982. Later his son Colm also represented Meath as a Fianna Fáil TD.

KEENAN, PADDY

Born in Trim, 1950. A leading exponent of the uileann pipes. A member of the Bothy Band in the 1970s, he has recorded a number of albums both with them and as a solo artist.

LEDWIDGE, FRANCIS

See under Francis Ledwidge.

MCDERMOTT, PETER

Born 1918. Gaelic footballer known as 'The Man in the Cap'. Won All-Ireland medals with Meath in 1949 and 1954 when he captained the side. Refereed All-Ireland Finals in 1953 and 1956. Coached Down to win the All-Ireland final in 1960. Pioneered the development of International Rules football when he brought Meath to Australia in 1967.

MOUNTCHARLES, LORD HENRY

See under Slane.

NANGLE, EDWARD

Born in Kildalkey in 1799. He was educated at Trinity College, Dublin to become a clergyman. Fired with evangelistic zeal, he founded a missionary settlement on Achill Island, Co. Mayo. His aim was to convert Catholics through setting up schools, a hospital, an orphanage and a printing-press which published the Achill Missionary Herald. His controversial methods brought the wrath of the Catholic clergy on him. The mission went into decline when Nangle left in 1852. He died in 1883.

O'CAROLAN, TURLOUGH

Although he spent his adult life out of Co. Meath, Turlough O'Carolan's birth near Nobber in 1670 and his early formative years in that area establish him as a genuine Meathman! When Turlough was fourteen his family moved to Co. Roscommon to work for the McDermott Roe household. The lady of the manor took an interest in the young lad's education, particularly when he was struck blind by small-pox at the age of eighteen. Mrs McDermott Roe had him taught the harp and O'Carolan readily took to playing and composing. At the age of twenty-one his patroness endowed him with a horse, a servant and some money and O'Carolan set out on a career as an itinerant harpist.

His travels took him around Connacht and Ulster, visiting the 'big houses' of chieftains and landlords. He would play and compose tunes for his patrons, particularly at weddings, wakes and funerals. He enjoyed great popularity and a visit to a particular area would draw many admirers. Many of his compositions were published in his own lifetime. Edward Bunting, the great 18th century collector of folk-music, included much of O'Carolan's work in his published volumes. Ultimately the great harpist's health deteriorated and he returned to Co. Roscommon where he died in 1738.

O'GROWNEY, FR. EUGENE

See under Athboy.

O'HIGGINS, AMBROSIO

Born near Dangan Castle in Summerhill in 1720. Emigrated to Peru as a teenager and worked his way up from being a pedlar to becoming an engineer in charge of road construction. Became a highly-respected figure in the Spanish colonial service, reaching its highest rank – Viceroy of Peru – in 1796. A province in Chile still bears his name. He died in 1810, and his son, Bernardo, liberated Chile from Spain but was later deposed and exiled to Peru.

O'HIGGINS, BRIAN

Born in Kilskyre, near Kells in 1882. He spent a lifetime promoting the Irish language and heritage as a writer and editor. He fought in the GPO during the Easter Rising of 1916 and was elected to the first Dáil as a member for Clare. He wrote many patriotic ballads and published the Wolfe Tone annual. He is particularly remembered in later life for his greeting cards which contained verses set in ornate Celtic designs. Died 1963.

O'REILLY, JOHN BOYLE

See under Dowth.

O'ROURKE, COLM

His origins may be in Leitrim, but he is acknowledged as the outstanding player in Meath football from the 1970s to the 1990s. A prolific scorer who was often a matchwinner for Meath, he is now a respected analyst for press and television.

PLUNKETT, ST. OLIVER

A member of the landed Plunketts of Loughcrew, he was born there in 1625. He studied for the priesthood in Rome, where he stayed on as lecturer because of the Cromwellian persecution at home. He eventually returned as Archbishop of Armagh in 1670 and set about re-organising the Irish church. He fell out with the Franciscan Order, then the largest order in Ireland. He became victim of a plot against him, which charged him with plotting a French invasion of Ireland. He was arrested in 1679 and after an abortive trial in Dundalk he was re-tried in London. Though clearly innocent, he was convicted and hanged at Tyburn in 1681. Oliver Plunkett was beatified in 1920 and canonised in 1975.

POYNTON, THOMAS

Born in Ballivor in 1801. He was not strictly an evangelist, but is credited with bringing the first priests to New Zealand, to where he emigrated via Australia, as a young man. He married a Wexford girl and they had three children. After each birth they sailed in an open boat to Sydney (a journey of 1200 miles) to have the child baptised. Each time Poynton made a plea to the Bishop of Sydney to appoint a priest for New Zealand. Poynton also wrote to the Pope for help and finally in 1838 three French missionaries arrived in New Zealand and the first Mass on New Zealand soil was celebrated in Poynton's home. He died in 1892 and is commemorated by a plaque at the site of his home in Carronstown, Ballivor.

SMYTH, BRIAN

Forever remembered as the captain of the team that won Meath its first All-Ireland Football title in 1949. He went on to win many further honours in both football and hurling, become an inter-county referee and has played a major role in a long career in the administration of Gaelic Games in Meath.

SMYTH, EDWARD

Born in Navan into a stone-cutting tradition in 1745. He studied stone-carving and was employed by James Gandon, the famous architect whose works include the Custom House, the Four Courts, the House of Lords and the King's Inns. Smyth worked with Gandon on all of these projects, carving the figure of Commerce at the Custom House and that of Moses at the Four Courts as well as other figures and coats of arms. His depiction of the Crucifixion of Christ hangs over the altar of St. Mary's Catholic Church in Navan. He died in 1812.

STEARNE, JOHN

Born in Ardbraccan near Navan in 1624, he studied medicine and became the first Professor of Medicine at Trinity College, Dublin. He was a founder of the College of Physicians and is regarded as one of the founding fathers of medical education in Ireland. Stearne died in 1665.

TULLY, JAMES

Politician. First elected as Labour TD for Meath in 1954 and though he lost out in the election of 1957, he came back in 1961 and represented Meath for the next twenty years. He held ministerial rank in coalition governments and had a lucky escape in 1981 when visiting Egypt as Minister for Defence. He was hit by shrapnel when sitting near President Sadat who was assassinated.

TULLY, FR. PATRICK

Born in Beauparc, he achieved fame as the coach of the Meath All-Ireland winning football teams in 1949 and 1954.

He was chairman of the Meath County Board of the GAA for a record twenty years. As a priest he served in Milltown (Westmeath), Moynalty and Duleek.

WELLESLEY, ARTHUR

Although born in Dublin in 1769, he was educated in Meath (Talbot's Castle, Trim) and later became MP for Trim as the Duke of Wellington. As a soldier, the 'Iron Duke' had a distinguished international career, culminating in the defeat of Napoleon at Waterloo in 1815. As a politician he rose through the ranks to become Prime Minister from 1828-30. During his term the Catholic Emancipation Act was passed in 1829, although he was personally opposed to it. He died in 1852 and his statue stands atop a huge memorial column in Trim.

WELLESLEY, RICHARD

Born in 1760. Elder brother of the Duke of Wellington, he was born at Dangan Castle, Summerhill. He entered politics and became Governor-General of India. He served two terms as Lord Lieutenant of Ireland and, unlike his brother, he was a supporter of Catholic Emancipation. Died in 1842.

In Praise of Meath

'Whether it be early spring or sultry summer or yellow autumn, there is still the same sylvan beauty, the ever changing tints which the green foliage, the graceful undulation of surface, the glancing river and the picturesque ruin impart to the landscape of these islands, nowhere else to be met with, whereon the eye never wearies, the mind never palls, and of which the memory never loses sight ...'

(The Beauties of the Boyne, William Wilde)

'I am always homesick. I hear the roads calling, and the hills, and the rivers wondering where I am ... If you go to Tara, go to Rath na Rí and look all around you from the hills of Drumconrath in the north to the plains of Enfield, where Allen bog begins and remember me to every hill and wood and ruin, for my heart is there ...'

(Letters from the Front to Katherine Tynan, Francis Ledwidge)

Yet lovely all the prospect seems
And suited to a poet's dreams
O'er all the verdure of the scene
Fresh sunbeams fling a brighter green;
Clouds of every shape and dye
Are scattered o'er the deep blue sky;
And melody of many a bird
In the charmed air is heard ...

(Verses on the Scenery of Trim, William Rowan Hamilton)

Dear Reader
This book is from our much complimented illustrated book series which includes:-

Belfast
By the Lough's North Shore
East Belfast
South Belfast
Antrim, Town & Country
North Antrim
Across the Roe
Inishowen
Donegal Highlands
Donegal, South of the Gap
Donegal Islands
Islands of Connaught
Sligo
Mayo
North Kerry
Fermanagh
Omagh
Cookstown
Dundalk & North Louth
Drogheda & the Boyne Valley
Meath
Fingal
Dublin's North Coast

Blanchardstown, Castleknock and the Park
Dundrum, Stillorgan & Rathfarnham
Blackrock, Dun Laoghaire and Dalkey
Bray and North Wicklow
Dublin 4
Limerick's Glory
Galway on the Bay
Connemara
The Book of Clare
Kildare
Carlow
Monaghan
Athlone
Cavan
Kilkenny
Armagh
Ring of Gullion
Carlingford Lough
The Mournes
Heart of Down
Strangford's Shores
Lecale

Cottage
Publications

Cottage Publications
is an imprint of
Laurel Cottage Ltd
15 Ballyhay Road
Donaghadee, Co. Down
N. Ireland, BT21 0NG

For details on these superb publications
and to view samples of the paintings they
contain, you can visit our web site
www.cottage-publications.com
or alternatively you can
contact us as follows:–
Telephone: +44 (0)28 9188 8033
Fax: +44 (0)28 9188 8063

We can also supply prints, individually signed by the artist, of the paintings
featured in many of the above titles as well as many other areas of Ireland.

For the more athletically minded our illustrated walking book series includes:–
Bernard Davey's Mourne   Tony McAuley's Glens
Rathlin, An Island Odyssey   Bernard Davey's Mourne Part 2

We also have an exciting new range which cover rivers in Ireland and includes:–
By the Banks of the Bann   The Liffey
My Lagan Love   Following the Foyle